Entrepreneurial Panacea:
Are we creating or destroying value?

CLAYTON FRASER WILLIAMS, MBA

COPYRIGHT © 2015

INTRODUCTION	**IX**

1 CHAPTER ONE: WHAT ARE WE TRYING TO ACHIEVE?	**1**
1.1 STUDY OUTLINE	4

2 CHAPTER TWO: LINKING ENTREPRENEURSHIP TO ECONOMIC GROWTH AND JOB CREATION	**5**
2.1 THE IMPORTANCE OF ECONOMIC GROWTH AND JOB CREATION. JOINT GOALS?	**6**
2.1.1 WHY IS ECONOMIC GROWTH IMPORTANT?	6
2.1.2 WHY IS JOB CREATION IMPORTANT?	9
2.2 ENTREPRENEURSHIP: INNOVATION, CAPITAL AND RISK	**11**
2.2.1 ENTREPRENEURSHIP: STARTING AT THE BEGINNING	12
2.2.2 INNOVATION, MORE THAN JUST A BUZZWORD	16
2.2.3 ANSWERING OUR FUNDAMENTAL QUESTION: WHO OR WHAT IS AN ENTREPRENEUR?	30
2.2.4 CAPITAL: A PRECURSOR TO ENTREPRENEURSHIP	34
2.2.5 RISK AND COST OF CAPITAL: THE CONSEQUENCES (AND REASONS) OF AND FOR EMPLOYING CAPITAL.	37
2.2.6 COST OF CAPITAL AND ECONOMIC GROWTH	39
2.2.7 LINKING INNOVATION, ECONOMIC VALUE ADDED AND ECONOMIC GROWTH	51
2.2.8 LABOUR	53
2.2.9 SMME OR ENTREPRENEUR?	57

3 CHAPTER THREE: WHAT ARE THE DRIVERS OF "ENTREPRENEURIAL SUCCESS"? 61

3.1 FINANCIAL CAPITAL 63
3.1.1 AN ACADEMIC REVIEW OF FINANCIAL CAPITAL AND ENTREPRENEURIAL SUCCESS 65
3.2 HUMAN CAPITAL 72

4 CHAPTER FOUR: WHY IS OUR CURRENT STRATEGY FOR PROMOTING SMMES FLAWED? 79

4.1 The importance of free market allocation of capital 79
4.2 What is wrong with increasing the supply of financial capital? 84
4.2.1 Cost of Capital and negative EVA ® 84
4.2.2 Increasing the supply of businesses that destroy economic value 86
4.2.3 Entrepreneurial agency theory 87
4.2.4 Unhealthy competition by exceeding market supply equilibrium: Promoting too Many Businesses and Destroying Entrepreneurship 88
4.2.5 Crowding out free market investors 92
4.3 Conclusion 94

5 CHAPTER FIVE: DEVELOPING A SOLUTION 95

5.1 DEVELOPING COMMERCIAL SKILLS: A MULTIDISCIPLINARY SET OF SKILLS REQUIRED COMBINE FACTORS OF PRODUCTION IN A WAY THAT REDUCES RISK AND MAXIMISES VALUE CREATION.   **96**
5.1.1   MARKET-LED RESPONSE: A LESS IMPERFECT SOLUTION   102
5.1.2   THE GOVERNMENT-LED RESPONSE WHEN THE MARKET FAILS   105
5.2 A STRATEGY FOR IDENTIFYING AND DEVELOPING TECHNICAL SKILLS 107
5.2.1   THEORY OF COMPARATIVE ADVANTAGE: HOW TO IDENTIFY A SECTOR FOR TECHNICAL SKILLS DEVELOPMENT   108
5.2.2   BALANCING THE TENSION BETWEEN CREATING ECONOMIC GROWTH AND CREATING JOBS   110
5.3 CONCLUSION   **117**
5.4 THE ELEPHANTS IN THE ROOM: UNPRODUCTIVE AND INFLEXIBLE LABOUR   **119**
5.4.1   MINIMUM WAGE   119
5.4.2   INFLEXIBLE LABOUR   122
5.4.3   THE INABILITY OF GOVERNMENT TO PROVIDE A BUSINESS ENVIRONMENT THAT IS CONDUCIVE TO SUCCESSFUL ENTREPRENEURSHIP   124

6   CHAPTER SIX: THE REST OF THE STORY   **127**

6.2 COST OF CAPITAL, ONLY PART OF THE STORY   **128**
6.3 HOW LONG?   **131**
6.4 AN IMPERFECT SOLUTION   **133**
6.4.1   COMPETING WITH PRIVATE ENTERPRISES IN THE PROVISION OF CAPITAL 134
6.4.2   TOO MANY MOTHS AROUND THE FLAME   134

6.5 OTHER IMPORTANT CONSIDERATIONS FROM OUR CIRCULAR-FLOW MODEL **137**
   6.5.1   EXPORTS AND IMPORTS   137
   6.5.2   GOVERNMENT SPENDING   142
   6.5.3   GOVERNMENT GRANTS   145
   6.5.4   EXPLAINING THE IMPORTANCE OF DEVELOPING VALUE CHAINS   147

7 CHAPTER SEVEN: CONCLUSION AND RECOMMENDATIONS 149

7.1   ADOPT A GREATER FREE MARKET APPROACH REGARDING FUNDING   153
7.2   FOCUS ON DEVELOPING QUALITY COMMERCIAL SKILLS WITHIN OUR ECONOMY   153
   7.2.1   IMPROVING THE QUALITY OF PRIMARY AND SECONDARY SCHOOLING   153
   7.2.2   RAISING THE STANDARD FOR ACCREDITATION OF COMMERCIAL/ENTREPRENEURIAL COURSES   154
   7.2.3   PUBLIC/PRIVATE PARTNERSHIPS   155
   7.2.4   IMPROVING THE QUALITY OF GOVERNMENT INSTITUTIONS THAT PROVIDE COMMERCIAL/ENTREPRENEURIAL EDUCATION   156
   7.2.5   EXPLOIT OPPORTUNITIES FOR ENTREPRENEURIAL DEVELOPMENT WITHIN VALUE CHAINS   156
7.3   FOCUS ON DEVELOPING QUALITY TECHNICAL SKILLS IN SECTORS THAT HOLD POTENTIAL FOR ACHIEVING OUR GOALS   158
7.4   FOCUS ON DEVELOPING THE TOURISM INDUSTRY   159
7.5   FOCUS ON GOVERNING WELL   160
   7.5.1   CORRUPTION   160
   7.5.2   CRIME   161
   7.5.3   GENERAL EFFICIENCY   161

7.5.4	SERVICE DELIVERY	162
7.5.5	LEGISLATIVE FRAMEWORKS	162
7.6	INCREASED PRODUCTIVE GOVERNMENT SPENDING	162
7.7	FOCUS ON SUBSIDISED INITIATIVES THAT WILL GET THE UNEMPLOYED INTO THE JOB MARKET	163
7.8	CONCLUSION	165
8	**BIBLIOGRAPHY**	**166**

Figure 1: Capital that contributes to economic growth and capital that detracts from economic growth — 44

Figure 2: Decreased returns due to subsidies — 45

Figure 3: Increased Cost of Capital due to Increased Entrepreneurial Failure at a Portfolio Level — 47

Figure 4: Combined Effects of Increased Cost of Capital & Reduced Returns — 48

Figure 5: Our focus must be on increasing entrepreneurs that contribute to economic growth by creating economic value — 49

Figure 6: Successful entrepreneurs contribute to economic growth — 52

Figure 7: The difference between entrepreneurs and SMMEs — 58

Figure 8: Cost of Capital typically increases as firm size decreases — 68

Figure 9: Smaller firms experience greater difficulty in accessing finance due to a higher cost of capital — 78

Figure 10: Free market funding will typically find its way to entrepreneurs that are likely to deliver returns greater than Cost of Capital — 80

Figure 11: Economic value destroyed by artificially increasing the supply of capital — 83

Figure 12: Artificially increased supply of capital increases number of SMMEs destroying economic value — 87

Figure 13: Market Equilibrium 89

Figure 14: Correlation between various sectors and either contribution to economic growth or job creation 115

Figure 15: Balance between economic growth and job creation 116

Figure 16: Government's contribution to destroying economic value 126

Figure 17: Entrepreneurs excluded from the economy due to administrative expenses 128

Figure 18: Justifiable subsidy based on administration costs 131

Figure 19: Justifiable subsidy should equal the value of government grants saved 147

INTRODUCTION

Unemployment is a persistent problem in South Africa, Africa and globally. If we want to address the inequality and poverty that plagues us, we will have to find solutions to the rising unemployment situation. This statement is nothing new. Since the advent of democracy, unemployment has been high on the agenda of the government. The buzzword "entrepreneurship" has become popular as government policy and practice has persistently sought to promote Small, Medium and Micro Enterprises (SMMEs) through various efforts of government in the hope that this will promote both economic growth and job creation. One of these practices has been increasing the amount of financial capital and subsidised capital available to SMME owners. Sadly, we see not only scant evidence of this strategy proving successful, but we see low levels of entrepreneurial activity, critically low economic growth, and a persistent rise in unemployment. Is our current strategy for allocating and subsidising financial capital destroying the value it seeks to create?

This book scrutinises these factors and their underlying assumptions to understand whether entrepreneurship holds promise for economic growth and job creation. If it does, we must understand what entrepreneurship is, how we are failing to promote it and how through promoting it, we can optimise its contribution not only to economic growth but specifically to job creation.

This book focuses on the South African example but applies to any emerging economy that is struggling with the challenge of unemployment and seeking to promote economic growth and job creation through entrepreneurship.

1 Chapter One: What are we trying to achieve?

As a nascent democracy, South Africa faces several challenges and elevated levels of unemployment underpin many of these challenges. Unemployment is certainly a "wicked problem" and one that has no obvious or simple solution. In the South African context, unemployment has its roots both in current economic conditions, as well as structural issues that began under the Apartheid Regime. Many of these structural issues have not been adequately addressed, while others such as education, have been perpetuated. Unemployment is thus a problem impacted by and impacting on several causal factors and social problems respectively, many of these being interrelated and forming positive feedback loops. Throughout this book, we must remind ourselves that the promotion of entrepreneurship or SMMEs is not a goal in itself. We are ultimately trying to address unemployment and entrepreneurship, if it is a solution at all, is simply a means to an end.

The need to find solutions to ameliorate unemployment is critical to several development goals in South Africa. These include goals that have been outlined in The Freedom Charter, The Constitution, The Reconstruction and Development Programme (RDP), Growth, Employment and Redistribution (GEAR), the New Growth Path (NGP) and The New Development Plan (NDP). While there are major ideological differences between the NGP and the NDP, both focus on unemployment and seek to promote entrepreneurship and Small, Medium and Micro Enterprises (SMMEs). The focus that the present government has placed on small businesses is evidenced by the New Business Development Act 2003 and more recently, the establishment of a new ministry for the development of small businesses in the executive.

The NGP, in particular, focuses on economic growth and a strong SMME sector as two key factors for addressing the problem of unemployment. These pillars are interlinked in that: It is assumed, based on economic theory, that elevated levels of economic growth (evidenced by the growth in GDP of between 5% and 7% per annum) will lead to a decline in unemployment. It is furthermore assumed that elevated levels of entrepreneurship and a strong SMME sector will both contribute to economic growth and directly impede unemployment through the creation of jobs. Yet, despite decades of focus on these areas, there is little evidence to suggest that these efforts are successful. Even in the years with strong economic growth, the percentage increase in jobs created did not keep pace with percentage increases in GDP per capita – giving South Africa an employment coefficient[1] of approximately 0.5. Currently, economic growth itself is unacceptably low. Furthermore, we see that entrepreneurial activity (as defined by the Global Entrepreneurship Monitor) remains low.

With such a "front of mind" focus on promoting entrepreneurship, why are the results so disappointing? This brings us to the nexus of the problem which is the focus of this book: Despite the allocation of prodigious amounts of financial capital, both subsidised and

---

[1] Defined as the ratio between percentage increase in employment and percentage increase in GDP.

unsubsidised, entrepreneurship levels remain low, economic growth continues to slow, and unemployment continues to escalate.

This book revisits some of the key assumptions underpinning the current approaches and seeks to answer the question: Is our current strategy for allocating and subsidising financial capital destroying the value it seeks to create?

With regards to our approach to addressing unemployment, this book proposes three hypotheses:

1. The subsidy of financial capital in South Africa is doing more to harm entrepreneurship, economic growth and job creation than it is to promote it.
2. The focus should be on increasing the supply of appropriate human capital, rather than financial capital within our economy.
3. A seven-point model is presented as a framework to assist us in better targeting our efforts to promote entrepreneurship that will lead to both economic growth and sustainable job creation.

We begin by trying to understand entrepreneurship and its notions that drive economic growth and job creation. We do this by exploring the origin of these notions and understanding the critical relationships between entrepreneurship, economic growth and job creation – both as joint and separate goals. Once these links are explicit, we can see where it is plausible to apply them and where they are applied incorrectly. From this point, I will be able to demonstrate why I believe that the approach of increasing the supply of capital to SMMEs both subsidised and unsubsidised, is inappropriate and doing more harm than good.

1.1 STUDY OUTLINE

This book consists of seven chapters. Following chapter one, which refocuses us on the problem that we are trying to solve, chapter two takes an in-depth look at entrepreneurship and its links to both economic growth and job creation. Chapter three explores the key drivers of entrepreneurial success. Chapter four explains why our current approach is destroying economic value and contributing to unemployment. Chapter five lays the foundation for us to develop a solution while Chapter Six explores further complications that must be considered in our solution. Chapter seven summarises and provides recommendations to develop a solution before concluding.

2 Chapter Two: Linking Entrepreneurship to Economic Growth and Job Creation

It is widely accepted in academic literature, government policy, and practitioner circles that entrepreneurship promotes both economic growth and job creation. Economic growth is important because it contributes to job creation. This is, in fact, so widely accepted that it is frequently stated without reference or evidence – implying that it is common sense.

This chapter explores the origins of these notions to put a solid case before the reader. It then reviews each of the elements of these theories that are essential to their individual validity. In doing so, we will see that it becomes important to understand exactly what is meant by entrepreneurship before applying or accepting the theory that the promotion of entrepreneurship will lead to either economic growth or job creation or both. At this point, we will see, for example, that it is important to distinguish between Small, Medium and Micro Enterprises (SMMEs) and entrepreneurs. This becomes the key theme of this book.

This chapter also introduces the financial, economic theory of Economic Value Added® developed by Prof Joel Stern of the University of Chicago, and applies it, as far as I can tell, for the first time to a macroeconomic level of a nationwide portfolio of SMMEs or entrepreneurs rather than only at a microeconomic level for a discrete firm. This sets the foundation for creating a theoretical link between entrepreneurship and economic growth. This, in turn, lays the foundation for understanding whether our current strategy for allocating and subsiding financial capital is destroying the value it seeks to create.

2.1 THE IMPORTANCE OF ECONOMIC GROWTH AND JOB CREATION. JOINT GOALS?

Before investigating whether the current allocation and subsidisation of financial capital is creating or destroying value, we must understand the reason for pursuing the goals of economic growth and job creation.

2.1.1 Why is economic growth important?

As stated in chapter one, our goal is to reduce unemployment. While not all economists agree that economic growth automatically translates into job creation, there is no disagreement with the fact that economic growth provides the means for creating jobs. In this book, it is accepted that economic growth does not necessarily create jobs automatically, but economic growth is recognised as a critical enabler of job creation.

When we talk about economic growth, we are typically referring to growth in the Gross Domestic Product (GDP) of an economy. Some economists prefer Gross National Income to Gross Domestic Product. Simplistically, Gross National Income is the Gross Domestic Product less the depreciation of the total national assets. For the point of this book, the difference is immaterial, and we will use Gross Domestic Product as the base metric for economic performance. Economic growth, measured as growth in GDP, is a function of population growth and the productivity of that population. Thus, a growing population with a constant level of productivity will experience growth in GDP or economic growth. From this, it follows that growth in GDP itself might not be useful. If for example a population grows rapidly and productivity declines slowly, it might be possible to maintain positive economic growth. It should be obvious to the reader that despite this growth in the GDP, the population on average will become poorer. This is because a substantially bigger population divides the slightly larger GDP. This gives rise to the concept of GDP per capita. The total Gross Domestic Product divided by the number of citizens in a population. In this book, therefore, a reference to economic growth, will refer specifically to growth in GDP per capita.

Very simplistically, GDP is the "size of the pie" and GDP per capita is the size of the slice given to each member of a population if the pie is divided equally. Unfortunately, we know that the pie is not distributed evenly among the South African population. This raises the question of distribution. In South Africa, a handful of the population gets very large slices of the pie while a large group get very little or nothing. The concepts of GDP, GDP per capita and distribution are very relevant to our problem of unemployment.

If some members of the population are unwillingly unemployed (they want to or must work, but can't find employment) we know that the pie is not being evenly distributed – regardless of how big the pie is or how high the GDP per capita is. This doesn't mean that the size of the pie (GDP) or its size relative to the size of the population (GDP per capita) is irrelevant. If our ultimate goal is to ensure that everyone gets a slice of the pie big enough to support them and their families, it is, of course, important that the pie is big enough to feed everyone. It is for this reason that GDP is important and with a growing population, why economic growth is important. GDP must grow at least as fast as the population just to maintain the current standard of living or a constant GDP per capita. One of the solutions to be able to distribute more to those who currently do not receive enough is to make sure that there is more to distribute. This means that the pie (GDP) must grow faster than the population or there must be a growth in GDP per capita. Returning to the fact that GDP is a function of the size of the population and the level of productivity of that population, it follows that if we want an increase in GDP per capita, that the population must become more productive. This is where innovation and entrepreneurship become important, but we will return to this point later. For now, we see that economic growth measured by an increase in GDP per capita means that we will have more to distribute. This means that we will have the means to create and sustain more jobs. Again, we return to the earlier point that growth in GDP per capita does not automatically create more jobs. We have seen earlier in this chapter that the recent history of South Africa proves that. This doesn't mean, however, that it is not a necessary factor for job creation, we have seen that it is; but there are others. This is what we mean by saying that economic growth is an enabler of job creation.

2.1.2 Why is job creation important?

This might appear to be a trivial question, but is it? Why are we trying to create jobs? To reduce poverty of course! Employment is a means of distribution. Going back to our pie, employment is a channel through which the pie can be distributed. There is more to it than that. Firstly, it is a means of distribution. Charity, social grants (the legal ones) and crime (on the illegal side of the scale) also contribute. These are all channels of distribution, and to the extent that employment is insufficient, the need for the other means of distribution will increase. Stated in other words - the less unemployment we have, the smaller the need for charity, social grants and crime. I won't spend any time on discussing why we want to reduce the use of crime as a channel of distribution, but I will explore why employment is a better channel of distribution than charity or social grants. The simple reason for this is reciprocity. At the most basic level, we assume that someone who is employed does something in return for the slice of the pie that they consume. Thus, the assumption is that they contribute to the overall size of the pie of which they are in part consuming. This is less true for recipients of charity or social grants. Obviously, the opposite is true for those engaged in crime - in taking their slice of the pie, they reduce the overall size of the pie.

We then see that job creation is not only means of distribution, but it is one that contributes to maintaining or possibly increasing the size of the national pie. More importantly, employment as a means of distribution contributes to the size of the slice (GDP per capita) available to each member of the population. We saw earlier that productivity is the ingredient for increasing GDP growth per capita or the size of the slice available to each citizen of a population. Each working member of society contributes to the productivity of that society. Each non-working member detracts from the productivity.

Thus, we see that job creation is not only a means of increasing distribution but also contributes to economic growth.

Therefore, it must be appreciated that authentic and sustainable job creation will contribute to economic growth.

We can see that our goals of economic growth and job creation are not mutually exclusive. They are enablers of each other, but it is important to understand that they are different and that by achieving the one, we do not automatically achieve the other. With this established, we must understand how, if at all, entrepreneurship contributes to economic growth and job creation. Once we understand this, we will be able to understand whether the current efforts to promote a strong SMME sector are promoting entrepreneurship, economic growth, and job creation.

2.2 Entrepreneurship: Innovation, Capital and Risk

As previously stated it is commonly accepted that the entrepreneurship contributes to both economic growth and job creation. This has translated into a strong focus on promoting SMMEs in the South African economy in the hope that this will drive economic growth and job creation. We have also seen, however, that the results have been disappointing at best. Where have we gone wrong? Or were we just wrong to begin with?

The first crucial link to understand is the one between entrepreneurship and both economic growth and job creation. To do this, we need to understand entrepreneurship. This is not easy since academics and practitioners alike do not always agree on what entrepreneurship is and are often ambiguous about it. To be sure, the definition that I will settle on in this book might be contested by many, but it must be understood in the context of our stated goal: Using entrepreneurship as a means to promote economic growth and job creation. For this reason, I arrive at this definition at working backwards from these goals: economic growth and job creation.

2.2.1 Entrepreneurship: Starting at the beginning

The concept of an entrepreneur (not always the term) can be traced back at least to the 18th century and is found in the works of economists such as Robert Reich, Richard Cantillon and Adam Smith. At the time entrepreneurship was something studied by economists. More recently, perhaps starting with Peter Drucker in the mid-20th century, entrepreneurship has become a field of study in itself. It is now studied and debated by economists, management experts and psychologists, to name but a few. It is also a buzzword that is used with much hype and little understanding among ultracrepidarians. In the mire of views and research on the subject, it is very easy to get lost and miss the proverbial wood for the trees. We will return to explore this in more depth shortly. For now, we must remember that we are looking for a link between entrepreneurship and both economic growth and job creation. Once we understand what it is about entrepreneurship that provides this link, we can explore the concept of entrepreneurship in more detail. We start by returning to the notion that entrepreneurship promotes economic growth. Joseph Schumpeter with his concept of creative destruction famously made this notion explicit. Much of this was implicit, however, in earlier writings such as *The Wealth of Nations* by Adam Smith.

2.2.1.1 Introducing the key ingredient of Innovation: Joseph Schumpeter and Adam Smith

In the context of a prevailing view in Schumpeter's time that Capitalism and big businesses were harmful to society, Schumpeter argued that the process of creative destruction engaged in by entrepreneurs led to economic development and growth that benefitted society more than it harmed it. It was out of this that the popular notion that entrepreneurship drives economic growth would be established. The focus of Schumpeter's argument here was innovation. Schumpeter believed that in the pursuit of profits, entrepreneurs would engage in research and development that would lead to new products that would make society, as a whole more, productive and would increase the standard of living for society as a whole. It is interesting to note that Schumpeter argued that big businesses were better positioned for this since they could afford to allocate capital to research and development. Here we have our first conflict with the concept that SMMEs are entrepreneurial. We will return to this later as there is a lot more to unpack in Schumpeter's argument than meets the eye.

We will remember that economic growth was a function of the increase in population size and the productivity of that population. When economic growth is measured in growth in GDP per capita, this is a direct function of the increase in productivity of the population. Schumpeter highlights for us, at least in part, how entrepreneurship contributes to economic growth. According to Schumpeter, the process of creative destruction improves the productivity of society by destroying old, less productive means and creating new ways of doing things that are more productive. This was central to Adam Smith's explanation of how industrialisation and the division of labour made society more productive and therefore increased the wealth of that society or, in today's economic language, led to an increase in GDP per capita.

By returning to Smith, we see innovation being split implicitly into two categories.

The first category is the one that Schumpeter was talking about, new technology that allows us to be more productive. In Adam Smith's day and even in Schumpeter's day, technology was typically industrial. Today, technology is often synonymous with Information and Communications Technology (ICT). In either case technology - whether new machines for farming (think of moving from ploughing by hand to ploughing with oxen to ploughing with a tractor) or new machinery to make nails as in one of Smith's many examples, or the internet and laptop computers – increases the productivity of a population, society or nation.

The second category is not necessarily a function of technology but refers to the way we do business. This was implicit in Adam Smith's "division of labour" which caused an entire revolution. The division of labour, however, was simply an innovation in the way of doing business that made it more productive. Often new technologies enable new ways of doing business more productively, but this is not always the case. An outstanding example of innovation in the way of doing business was the McDonald's model. There were no new technologies involved, there were no new products involved – the hamburger had been around for a very long time. What McDonald's did was to apply the concepts of division of labour, the ensuing concept of a production line, standardisation and a few existing technologies into the production of hamburgers. In doing this, they managed to deliver an existing product in significantly less time and at a fraction of the cost than originally done. By lowering the cost of an existing product, McDonald's increased the purchasing power of its market (they could buy more with the same money) or produce more with the same labour, which as Smith pointed out is the same thing, and thereby increased the wealth of their target market. To return to Schumpeter without leaving this example:

By producing an existing product at less cost, McDonald's forced their competitors to rethink the way they did business. They either had to emulate this new efficiency or redefine their value proposition in the market. This is an example of creative destruction. The creation of a new, more efficient way of doing things steadily destroyed less efficient ways of producing the same product. To use a microeconomic concept: McDonald's ability to supply the burger at a lower price meant that the demand for their product increased. This both allowed McDonald's to replicate their more efficient means of production and forced competitors to find a way to supply competing products at similar prices (or go out of business). The total effect of this was to supply the cheaper product to an increasingly wider population, thus increasing the purchasing power or wealth of that population.

Thus, the short answer to our question is that entrepreneurship contributes to economic growth by increasing productivity through innovation. By finding more productive ways of doing business, or by bringing new products to the market that allow other businesses to function more productively or society, or parts of society to be more productive. There are two problems with this answer. Firstly, we haven't explicitly linked entrepreneurship to innovation. Secondly, we have seen how entrepreneurship can contribute to economic growth or the creation of wealth, but we haven't explicitly seen how it contributes to job creation or the distribution of newly created wealth. On the contrary, one could plausibly argue (and many do) that the introduction of new technologies and new ways of doing business reduce the demand for labour, thus causing an economy to shed jobs. We will return to this issue, but first, we must understand exactly what innovation is.

2.2.2 Innovation, more than just a buzzword

Having been a so-called "tier one" strategy consultant, myself, buzzwords, and consulting jargon are my *bête noire*. This is not because I do not use phrases like "mutually exclusive and collectively exhaustive" or innovation. Not at all. My distaste stems from the ignorant use of the buzzwords and phrases to mask the reality that the person using them has not a clue what they are talking about. This promiscuous use of buzzwords and phrases tends to diminish their importance. Next time you hear someone talking about innovation, politely ask them to explain what they mean.

Returning to the point, however: We have seen that there are essentially two types of innovation. Innovation that brings new products or technologies to the market, and innovation that introduces more productive ways of bringing existing products to markets. As simple as the concept of innovation is, this does not fully explain what innovation is – at least not in the context of entrepreneurship.

Innovation is not just the development of a new technology or a new business model. That is invention, and it is only half of the story. Innovation is the successful commercialisation of a new technology, product, idea, or way of doing business. The difference is subtle, but crucial nonetheless. The successful commercialisation of something new has one very important implication: In economic terms, there is a demand for the new technology, product, idea, or way of doing business. In marketing terms, we are creating value for the customer. From an economic point of view, this takes us straight back to Adam Smith's explanation of the microeconomics of supply and demand. What this means is that the market decides whether our innovation adds value. From a practical point of view, it emphasises a critical and often overlooked truth about innovation and entrepreneurship: It is business and the commercial aspect cannot and should not be neglected. I could write an entire book on this aspect, but I will limit the commentary to a few short, sharp insights.

The commercialisation aspect of innovation is critical to entrepreneurship. There are countless examples of superior technologies that have failed to be successful while similar inferior technologies have succeeded. The light bulb is only one of these examples. Edison's light bulb was not the most superior product from a technological standpoint, yet he succeeded where others failed. Not only did his succeed, but went on to lay the way for GE – one of the largest and most innovative companies in the world.

At first, the success of "inferior" products over "superior" ones might appear to be a travesty, but on closer inspection, we will see why this is not necessarily the case. It is also why so many would-be entrepreneurs fail. This is such an important point that I allow the small digression from the overall point of this book – primarily because it will contribute to our overall understanding of what type of entrepreneurship is needed to promote economic growth, but also because I believe that it is useful for entrepreneurs to understand this.

Technological superiority is not always superiority in economic terms. We can borrow from the concepts of the Pareto principle (80/20 principle) and the concept of the law of diminishing returns to understand this. In economic terms, 80% of the technological/product quality is often more than good enough for the market simply because this lowers the cost of bringing the technology or product to market to a point where it is affordable. 80% of the quality can be achieved with 20% of the cost or effort. To achieve the additional 20% of the quality can often increase the cost significantly – conceptually, it could add another

80% to the cost or effort required. In terms of the cost/benefit ratio means that this innovation simply does not add more value to society than its cost to society. Please note that when I talk about quality, I mean the quality as the standard of the product, not quality as defined in six sigma terms: the number of times that we manage to deliver specified quality. The latter, we know, drives costs down. The former drives cost up. This concept of only delivering the quality that the market is willing to pay for is a key premise of "Blue Ocean Strategy" and would almost seem obvious. Unfortunately, for entrepreneurs that are passionate about their product, it is often not obvious. Entrepreneurs often are far more passionate about the quality of their product than the quality that their customers care about. They assume that by having the very best, they will have a successful product. History has taught far too many entrepreneurs a very hard lesson this way.

In essence, a key factor of innovation is understanding exactly what the market demands and supplying exactly that at the price the market is willing to pay. Implicitly, this means being able to develop and deliver the product to the market in a manner that is efficient enough to ensure a margin between cost and price that will provide sufficient return on the various forms of capital required to bring the product to market. This concept of return on capital is equally critical and is central to the message of this book. We will thus, return to this later in this chapter.

Concluding the concept of innovation, however, we see that innovation is about successfully commercialising a new technology, product, idea, or way of doing business. This means that the innovation must be something that the market demands and it must be brought to market at the price that the market is willing to pay. The costs involved in doing so must be sufficiently smaller than the price the market is willing to pay to ensure an acceptable return on the various types of capital for doing so. This means that:

- The innovation must be something the market wants – not something the entrepreneur wants the market to want.
- The entrepreneur (and his/her management team) must be able to consistently manage the business in such a way that costs are under control while consistently delivering to the market the quality and quantity that the market demands.

This is all forms part of successful innovation.

Another critical aspect of innovation is the constant renewal. Too often entrepreneurs successfully commercialise a product and then build what they think is a business around that product. They enjoy strong margins due to their first mover advantage but start flailing when competitors move in on their market. Often, they have not got their costs under control because they have enjoyed such strong margins in the initial stages of the product lifecycle. Their competitors, however, do get their costs under control and take business away. This shortens the life of their product's "s-curve". The entrepreneur can extend the life of their product curve by keeping costs under control, but even so, at some point, they are going to have to either improve their product through sustaining innovation or completely cannibalise their product and bring another new product to the market. Firms like 3M, Proctor and Gamble and GE do this well as do the automobile manufacturers. Too many entrepreneurs hold onto their first success with everything they have – only to lose everything they have.

All the above is critical because it will ensure that innovation is commercially successful enough to provide a return on the full combination of capital that is required to bring the innovation to the market. Another concept implicit in Schumpeter's argument was that investment is a critical enabler of innovation. This is why Schumpeter argued that big firms are better positioned for innovation: They have more resources to invest in research and development.

For now, we have seen how innovation contributes to economic growth through what Schumpeter called creative destruction. Innovation makes an economy more productive, either through producing more with less and thereby increasing purchasing power or by creating new demand. The market is the judge of what will and what will not make society or an economy more productive. What we have not seen and what Schumpeter did not explain, is whether innovation leads to job creation. It is implicit in his argument that society shares in the benefits of innovation and this can happen without job creation. If innovation increases the productivity of a society and thereby increases the purchasing power of that society, it means that even without creating more jobs it increases the wealth of the society by increasing the purchasing power of their existing labour. Thus, even without job creation, innovation is important. We will explore whether innovation can lead to job creation as well as economic growth.

2.2.2.1   Does innovation create or destroy jobs?

The answer is that it can do both. From a macroeconomic point of view, we are interested in whether the net effect is positive or negative: Does innovation create more jobs than it destroys? Before we answer this, it is important to understand that the destruction of jobs is not an issue of little consequence and that this is a big consideration for policy makers. Often finding the balance between job creation and job destruction is difficult. This is because those who lose their jobs cannot necessarily move from their obsolete job to one of the new jobs. A simple conceptual example of this is where machines replace manual labour in either manufacturing or agriculture. The introduction of a new technology that displaces 5000 jobs might be offset by another innovation that creates 10 000 jobs. If the new jobs need a skill that the 5000 unemployed do not have, they will not be able to move into the new jobs without training. Very often they might be too old, or might just not have the aptitude to acquire the new set of skills required. Alternatively, they might not have the means to afford the training, or the new jobs might not coincide with their geographic location and relocation might not be an option. John Maynard Keynes had this to say about the effect of technological innovation, the ensuing increase in productivity and its effect on labour:

"We are suffering, not from the rheumatics of economic slow-down, but from the growing pains of overly rapid changes from the painfulness of readjustment between one economic period and another. The increase of technical efficiency has been taking place faster than we can deal with the problem of labour absorption. For the moment, the very rapidity of these changes is hurting us and bringing difficult problems to solve. We are being afflicted with a new problem of which some readers may not yet have heard the name, but which they will hear a great deal in the years to come – namely, technological unemployment. This means unemployment due to our discovery of means of economising the use of labour outrunning the pace at which we can find new uses for labour."

This is a critical consideration that we must understand, but which this book does not pretend to solve for. The first step is to understand how innovation can create jobs, how it can destroy jobs and whether the net result is positive or negative.

The easiest to understand is how innovation can destroy jobs. The introduction of a new technology can simply make jobs obsolete. In the South African context mechanisation is just one example of this. Whether it is mechanised harvesting in agriculture or forestry or mechanised mining, we end up with a situation where more jobs are destroyed than created. The mechanisation would not take place if it were not economically viable to do so. Thus, we can assume fairly safely that this innovation is creating economic value at a macroeconomic level, but it is distorting the distribution of that value even more than it currently is.

This is a real problem, in truth a "wicked problem": one that has no easy solution and sadly this is beyond the scope of this book. I will submit that if we can create more wealth (which we have seen we can), and if we can create more jobs than we destroy (we will explore whether this is a possibility), then we will at least be in a strong position to address the needs of those whose unwilling sacrifice has served the greater good. Put differently: As difficult as it is, we should guard against perpetuating a situation where we do not have sufficient means to sustain the entire population, let alone enough channels to distribute those means, simply to avoid confronting this difficult problem.

Does innovation create more jobs than it destroys? The answer is, unfortunately, not definite and is certainly not simple. The answer is that it can and generally does in the long-run. The easiest way to understand this is to look back at history. The first major innovation that was disruptive was the advent of agriculture. Over a period, this changed societies from being hunter-gatherers to being farmers. The changes were enormous: People started living in cities, a larger population could be supported, and a larger number of people who were not economically active could be supported. This led to more leisure time, which led to innovations such as writing and crafting. Value chains were expanded, and more jobs were created in the value chain of making agricultural implements, building permanent structures, etc. There are two very critical points here, however: The first is that this happened over a long period of time. It took society time to adjust to innovation. One of the reasons for this is the second point. The job of hunter-gatherers became less important, and almost certainly, several hunter-gathering "positions" (conceptually) were made obsolete. Several hunter-gatherers had to change their entire way of life and settle down to become farmers.

The next major period of disruptive innovation was the industrial revolution (of which Keynes was writing). This over-simplifies history as there were countless innovations in the thousands of years that transpired between these periods, not to mention the wheel, ships, the compass, etc. Our objective is to view the impact of innovation on society – not to give a detailed account of history. The industrial revolution radically disrupted life, as it was known. Over a period of time society moved from agriculture to industry. We can see, for example in the novels of Dumas, Austin, Balzac and even in Dicken's novels, that concept of capital (wealth) was generally associated with land (which could be used or rented out for agriculture). We know that this is very different from our view of capital (wealth) today. This shift has happened because of innovation, first the industrial revolution and latterly, the IT revolution (and thousands of innovations in-between). Each period of innovation has, in the short-term, undoubtedly destroyed jobs. In the long-run, however, it is nearly impossible to refute that the innovations have created jobs. 300 years ago, there were no jobs for pilots, computer programmers, auditors, safety officers, genetic researchers, welders, etc.

Furthermore, there were far fewer jobs for the likes of teachers, accountants, and clerks. The growing population has increased the need for several jobs, but there are at least three other factors that have made job opportunities possible. Firstly, the wealth created through the increased productivity that innovation has afforded us has given us the means to demand or be able to afford these services. Secondly, innovation has directly created many of these jobs. Thirdly, the increased productivity in one part of society (due to innovation) has created a demand in another part of society that has led to the creation of jobs. This latter statement is easy to gloss over without much notice, but it is critical to the focus of this book: The increased productivity in one part of society (due to innovation) has created a demand in another part of society. This demand, when not supplied, is an opportunity and it is the entrepreneurs that respond to this opportunity. Thus, it is the entrepreneur that plays a critical role in helping society to adjust to the changes brought about by the innovation of other entrepreneurs. This is fact is too important to neglect, because this introduces the concept of risk which, as we will see, forms part of entrepreneurship, but it also explains how free markets are critical to allow entrepreneurs to create jobs and contribute to economic growth. Note that I have for the first time, put the concept of job creation ahead of economic growth. Before we explore this, we must conclude our discussion on how innovation can create jobs. I have both inadvertently and deliberately let the cat out of the bag on this one.

Innovation is almost always incomplete in the sense that it often creates other wants and needs. The innovation of using an aircraft for transport led to the need for increased reliability, safety, carrying capacity and speed. This, in turn, created needs for bigger airports, better jet (technically turbofan) engines, better baggage handling facilities, better materials for tyres, airframes and engines and more comfortable seats. The value added to society, along with countless other innovations that increased the productivity and therefore the wealth of society, meant that these demands could be met. This provided opportunities for entrepreneurs to build businesses around these innovations and as the demand grew, these businesses grew and created jobs. As competition increased, these businesses had to focus on business model innovation. Examples of these were the production line and the use of standardisation to build the model-T Ford, the "Lean" system made famous by Toyota. Lean has been successfully (and unsuccessfully) replicated in hundreds, if not thousands of industries. One outstanding example is that of supermarkets, the most famous example of which is Walmart. Walmart used business model innovation to change the way people's shopping needs were met, and in the process, both increased the wealth of society by increasing the purchasing power of society through efficiency and created thousands of jobs. Walmart destroyed jobs among competitors, but it created more jobs than it destroyed. This was not only because it could afford to, but also because doing so increased its profits, which unwittingly added to the overall wealth of society. Today, the Amazon model is replacing the Walmart-model, and Walmart is responding by adapting their model to stay relevant. So, the creative destruction continues. These innovations not only created wealth and jobs but also other needs that could be met by entrepreneurs. The successful ones would go on to create further wealth and more jobs. It is impossible to argue against the fact that more people are gainfully employed today than could have been employed 100 years ago. Innovation has played a crucial role in this, as has the entrepreneur who has brought about these innovations. Many have failed, many have lost fortunes, and much more have lost jobs. The beauty of the free market and entrepreneurship, however, is that each of these failures has presented an opportunity. Not only have entrepreneurs played a central role in creating economic growth and in creating jobs, but they have played an indispensable role in restoring the balance when a shift in the labour market has been caused by innovation. The process is not perfect, and in the short-term, there are many losers. These losses are real and painful and worthy of serious attention, but often the desperate need brought about by such losses is exactly the catalyst needed to bring about the next innovation that is needed to reverse these losses.

Thus, we have seen that, in the system in which we operate, innovation does create wealth and economic growth and it both creates and destroys jobs, but also that history very strongly suggests that more jobs are created than destroyed. This is probably driven more by our need for employment (to earn a living) than as a pure consequence of innovation. It is through innovation that these jobs are created, and the movement from obsolete jobs to new jobs occurs. While we opened with innovation, it has been impossible not to introduce the role of the entrepreneur. If innovation is the successful commercialisation of new technologies, products, ideas, and business models, then the entrepreneur, at least by the definition implied in our preceding discussion, is the individual who commercialises these technologies, products, ideas, and business models. In doing so and almost always in the pursuit of monetary gain, the entrepreneur inadvertently contributes to the greater good of society through economic growth (the creation of wealth) and job creation (the distribution of that wealth). This is not because of his/her intention to do so (at least not in most cases), but because of their pursuit of profit. This is almost a paraphrase of Adam Smith who famously wrote: *"It is not from the benevolence of the butcher, the brewer, or the baker that we expect our dinner, but from their regard to their own interest".*

Again, this can (and does) open an enormous debate about whether this is the best approach. Additionally, we do see more and more altruism in many entrepreneurial pursuits and the advent of social entrepreneurship: The pursuit of profit because of benevolence is becoming more prolific. Ultimately, however, even social entrepreneurship is not entrepreneurship without a profit. How that profit is made is certainly a topic worthy of discussion, as is the distribution of that profit, as is the discussion about whether profit should be our only goal. These aside, profit remains an indispensable aspect of entrepreneurship. In my opinion, the responsible pursuit of a profit that is fairly distributed with due consideration for all stakeholders is not only necessary but also good. This is subject matter for another book perhaps, for now, we have gotten ahead of ourselves. We first need to understand what an entrepreneur is.

2.2.3 Answering our fundamental question: Who or what is an entrepreneur?

"A person who makes money by starting or running businesses, especially when this involves taking financial risks." – *Oxford Advanced Learners Dictionary*.

This is a good starting point and gives us many of the key elements common to many of the academic discussions. It tells us that an entrepreneur is someone who:

1. Makes money
2. Starts or runs a business
3. Takes financial risk to achieve number 1 and by doing number 2

According to the economic definition, the entrepreneur combines other factors of production (natural resources, labour and capital) to produce finished goods or services, implicitly at a profit.

Entrepreneurship was initially a concept used by economists and, as far as we can tell was first used early in the 18th century by the French economist, Richard Cantillon. According to Cantillon, the entrepreneur takes risk by combining resources (now called factors of production) to maximise financial return. The key to his definition was the concept of risk in dealing with uncertainty in pursuit of profit. He very clearly delineated between the entrepreneur and the provider of capital. Later in the 18th century, another French economist, Jean Baptiste-Say, introduced the concept of increasing the productive function of resources as a key function of the entrepreneur. Later, John Stuart Mill and Adam Smith both explored the concept of entrepreneurship and included risk due to uncertainty in their discussions. What they did differently from Cantillon is blur the lines between the capitalist as a provider of capital and the entrepreneur. The greatest change to this definition came from Joseph Schumpeter in the 1930's who proposed that innovation was key to entrepreneurship and we have covered this new aspect in great detail. Essentially, what Schumpeter contributed was that the entrepreneur innovated by doing one of the following or a combination of the thereof:

1. Developing new products or services
2. Developing new ways of producing existing products or services
3. Identifying or developing new markets for existing products or services
4. Identifying new sources of supply for the production of products or services
5. Developing new forms of organisations

Most importantly, Schumpeter believed that the entrepreneur did not bear risk. The capitalist or the provider of capital bore risk. This broke with Mills, Smith, and contemporary economists, but was congruent with the proposition put forward by Cantillon.

More recently, Peter Drucker and Frank Knight have returned to the concept that the entrepreneur is a risk taker.

Personally, I believe that there is no single truth on the matter. It is beyond doubt that the provider of capital (if this is not the entrepreneur, and in most cases, it is not) bears risk. The entrepreneur, even if he or she is not the provider of capital, bears risk. About the concept of innovation, I believe that this is a critical element for the purposes of our focus: economic growth and job creation. The degree of innovation will differ from business to business, but some form of innovation will be needed if the entrepreneur is to be successful. Again, we need to return to what Schumpeter meant by innovation. This was not just limited to new products and services, or new technologies. This could be as simple as identifying a new (unsupplied) market. The entrepreneur that successfully supplies an unmet demand will have the opportunity of earning a financial return and will contribute to economic growth and job creation.

Recently, entrepreneurship has also become the domain of psychologists who analyse the personality traits of an entrepreneur, such as internal locus of control, risk-taking propensity, and the need for achievement. I do not dismiss these as unimportant, but I have not included them in this book as they are less relevant to the challenges that we are trying to overcome.

Let us first build our definition of what an entrepreneur is if we state that an entrepreneur must contribute to economic growth and job creation.

The entrepreneur pursues profit. Later in this chapter, I will define profit as economic profit or Economic Value Added, and in this way, we not only fully understand what we mean be profit, but we will also be able to link it to economic growth. Again, I am happy to accept that increasingly entrepreneurs today are doing this through increasingly benevolent means than Adam Smith spoke of and that less and less of the pursuit of profit is purely out of self-interest. Notwithstanding, however, self-interest to some degree will always play a role and more importantly, the pursuit of profit – even if pursued alongside other goals, is critical. The distribution of these profits is all-together a different question. Given the framework of labour law in South Africa, as well as the fact that we, for the most part, are world-class in terms of corporate governance (at least in the private sector), I am going to assume that profits are mostly fair and that when jobs are created, these are fairly remunerated. I am willing to accept that this is not always the case, but this is not a problem that falls within the scope of this book. To pursue a profit, the entrepreneur must combine resources or factors of production to produce a product or service (or combination and range thereof) to supply a demand in the market. In doing so, there is definitely risk involved. In the process, the entrepreneur contributes to economic growth through innovation and by increasing the productivity of the resources or factors of production combined, and as the entrepreneurs' business grows, he/ she creates jobs.

We have taken the long road to arrive at this definition, but it is important that we understand each of the elements in great detail, so that we can answer another important question: Is it possible for entrepreneurs to destroy economic value? Of course, the answer that any economist will give you: It depends. Notwithstanding, however, the answer in this book is no. This is more as a result of the convenient way in which I define an entrepreneur. Since I have worked backwards from our goals of economic growth and job creation, the entrepreneur, by the definition that I have arrived at, is someone who contributes to these. We will see how in the remainder of this chapter. Before I answer this, I want to address the issue of size. In truth, I am less interested in size than I am in addressing the issue that the term SMME is used interchangeably with the term entrepreneur. I believe, for reasons that I will discuss at the end of this chapter, that this is one of our critical failings in addressing unemployment. We are focused on the wrong thing. Before we address this question, we need to explore one more element of our definition: Capital.

2.2.4 Capital: A precursor to entrepreneurship

Capital is not part of an entrepreneur, but capital is a critical factor in an entrepreneur's success. Capital is as integral to what an entrepreneur does as what land is to what a farmer does. I am sure that there will be one reader that can think of an example where a farmer does not need any land, but for the purposes of this book, I will ask that we accept the general rule that to farm, a farmer needs land. Some need more than others, depending on a wide array of conditions. Similarly, an entrepreneur needs capital. Importantly, according to many of the economists, the accumulation of capital is also critical to economic growth. Keynes attributes economic growth to both innovation (technological advancement) and the accumulation of capital. Importantly, capital only contributes to economic growth when productively employed. It is the entrepreneur who employs capital productively in pursuit of (economic) profit. We will see in the following two sections of this chapter that the economic profit or Economic Value Added is the measure of how productively capital is employed.

According to the economic definition, an entrepreneur combines factors of production in the pursuit of profit. One of these factors of production is capital. Looking at the definitions of Cantillon, Baptiste-Say and Smith – one of the common threads is that an entrepreneur employs capital and incurs risk in doing so. They might be divided on who bears the risk, but the common thread is that the entrepreneur employs capital in pursuit of a profit and does so at risk.

The obvious question is, what is capital? The reader should anticipate by now that economists do not have one definite answer. This is because capital is context specific. I am going to cheat therefore and explain capital as a concept rather than as a definite article. Capital, as a broad concept, is everything except labour and natural resources that are employed in the production of finished goods or services. (Even so, capital is needed to maintain employed labour and natural resources – this forms part of our "working capital"). This was central to the arguments of all the classical economists. Thus, capital would include the stock in a supermarket (generally working capital), buildings employed for profit, or factories and machinery employed in production (generally fixed capital). The common denominator is that capital needs to be purchased or, at the very least, has financial value. This is why capital has a financial connotation. Financial capital is, of course, money, but it is money that is earmarked for investment or to be employed in production. Once financial capital is used to purchase something for producing goods or services to be sold at a profit, it is no longer financial capital, but it is still capital either fixed or working. According to Thomas Piketty, a French economist and author of *Capital in the 21st Century*, capital is something that can be bought or sold. For this reason, Piketty disagrees with the concept of Human Capital as introduced by Gary Becker. For the purpose of this book, this disagreement is technical and immaterial, but we will explore the concept of human capital later. For now, we will accept that capital implicitly speaks of finance, since finance is almost certainly a prerequisite for acquiring capital unless the capital is accumulated, inherited, or donated in a form other than financial capital. Even in this latter case, it would have been purchased with money at some point. Returning to the definition of the entrepreneur provided, the entrepreneur employs capital for a profit and risks the capital in doing so. This risk requires a reward, which leads us to the concept of a return on capital.

2.2.5 Risk and Cost of Capital: The consequences (and reasons) of and for employing capital.

In both the "The Wealth of Nations" by Adam Smith and *Kapital* by Karl Marx there are two key elements that demand a return: capital and labour. We will return to labour shortly.

Why does capital demand a return?

When capital is employed by the entrepreneur, the capital is put at risk. Plainly, the entrepreneurial venture could fail, and the capital could be diminished or lost. So why risk your capital? The only reason is that there is a chance that the capital can be increased. The greater the risk to the capital, the greater the return expected. It is important to understand that the providers of capital have options and that these options are governed by the same supply and demand rules that govern any market. The supplier of capital meets a demand for capital at a price level that is a function of risk, supply and demand. The market price of capital is the cost of capital.

Let us consider a supplier of capital supplying capital at zero risk. US government bonds are a good example of zero risk. This is because the supplier of capital supplies (lends) a certain amount of capital to the US government who guarantees to pay back the capital at the end of a period. The chances of the US government not repaying this debt are considered to be as close to zero as one can get. As a result, the interest rate (return on capital) paid to the supplier of the capital is very low. This interest rate is not only a function of the risk, however. If the US government is in need of borrowing large sums, it will have to pay a higher price (interest rate) to borrow the capital, and interest rates will go up. If the demand declines, the interest rates will be lower. This is an oversimplification, but it provides us with a good example of the cost of capital. The government bond interest rate is often referred to as the risk-free rate and should, in a stable economy, typically reflect the inflation rate. This is because the supplier of capital will want to receive the same real value (nominal value adjusted for inflation) as the amount that was supplied. Thus, with government bonds, the real cost of capital is close to zero. The nominal cost is close to the inflation rate.

The next important concept about the return on capital is the market is risk premium. This is when a supplier of capital invests their money in the market. In the South African context, this would mean buying a balanced portfolio of all the shares on the Johannesburg Stock Exchange (JSE). This would expose the supplier of capital to the risk of the entire JSE and would equally expose them to the potential returns of the JSE. This is clearly riskier than buying government bonds, and for this reason, the return is expected to be higher. The difference between the return expected by the market and the risk-free rate is known as the market risk premium. Typically, investments are compared to the expected market return. Entrepreneurial investments are riskier than an investment in the market. Consequently, the expected return is higher. This means that the cost of capital is higher.

Let us for a moment assume that an investor supplies capital to a firm (by buying its shares on the JSE) that is twice as risky as the market. In technical terms, we would say that this share has a beta of two because it is twice as risky as the market. Now let us assume that this investor only receives a return that is equal to the risk-free rate. Remember that the investor is being paid the risk-free rate for the supplied capital when the business that is using the capital is exposing the investor to twice the risk of the market with regard to losing the capital or having it reduced. Clearly, this investor is underpaid and would be better off buying risk-free government bonds and earning the same return.

This is analogous to renting out a seven-bedroom house in a good area at the same price as someone renting out a two bedroom flat in an average area. Clearly not a good idea, one would be losing money.

2.2.6 Cost of Capital and Economic Growth

The concept of the cost of capital is critical in understanding how entrepreneurship would contribute to economic growth.

Capital is a finite and scarce resource, and there is competition for it. This means that it commands a premium. The supplier of capital expects a return in the same way as someone expects rent from the tenants using his or her house. In fact, the house is a form of capital (fixed capital), and the rent is the return on the capital. If we view capital as a product that is both supplied and demanded we understand the cost of capital quite easily. The cost of capital is a function of the risk to the capital as well as the supply and demand. The greatest influence on the cost of capital, however, is the risk. This is because the supply and demand are relatively stable.

When the capital does not earn a return equal to or greater than its risk-related cost of capital, economic value is destroyed. When capital earns a return equal to its cost of capital, economic value is maintained. When capital earns a return greater than its cost of capital, economic value is created.

More simply: Capital is finite, but can be increased, maintained, or decreased. The risk is the chance that the capital, over a period of time, will suffer loss. This is the cost of using that capital in the specific way that generates the risk. Thus, the cost of capital is the return that ensures that all losses will be compensated over the period and the capital will be maintained. This means that when a return on capital is lower than the cost of employing that capital, the capital will decrease.

Thus, the cost of capital is just another expense of doing business, such as rent, salaries and wages, electricity, etc. A firm that is not earning at least the risk-adjusted and market-related cost of capital after all other operating expenses is not making a profit. It also means that this firm is reducing the capital stock of the country or economy in which it is owned and is, therefore, destroying economic value. It is also important to understand that the cost of capital is not just the cost of debt, but the total cost of all the capital invested in the firm including both debt and equity. It is thus the weighted average of the cost of debt and equity. To give an indication, the average returns of the JSE all-share index from 2003 to 2012 were 18.4%[2]. As a round number, no entrepreneurial venture should earn a return of less than 20% after all operating expenses have been deducted. Typically, higher risk entrepreneurial efforts (classically start-ups) might be expected to return anything between 25% and 40%, again after all operating expenses (including salaries for the owner/manager). This sounds high but is directly related to the riskiness of such ventures.

It is at this point that I believe it is important for us to understand the concept of economic profit or Economic Value Added or EVA® as developed by Prof Joel Stern of the University of Chicago and that we apply it for the first time (as far as I can tell) to the portfolio of SMMEs and entrepreneurs in an economy. While some might argue that EVA® is an antiquated measure of success and that it neglects a more holistic focus such as blended value that would include the triple bottom line I

---

[2] https://www.investec.co.za/research-and-insights/newsletters/monthly-view-newsletter/january-2013-articles/equity-markets.html

believe that it is a (not the only) critical measure and that it allows us to link the output of entrepreneurs directly to economic growth.

To reiterate, I do not believe that it should be the only measure of success; this will be demonstrated in the 7-point model suggested towards the end of this book.

Economic Value Added or EVA ® is the concept of economic profit applied at a firm level and is the Net Operating Profit *(NOPAT)* less the cost of capital *(C)*.

$$(NOPAT - C)$$

We understand from the Capital Asset Pricing Model (CAPM) that the cost of capital is the total weighted cost of debt and equity and we understand from that this is directly related to risk in a positive linear relationship.

Stern argues that when *NOPAT* is greater than *C* economic value is created (by a firm), but that when *NOPAT* is less than *C* economic value is destroyed (by a firm).

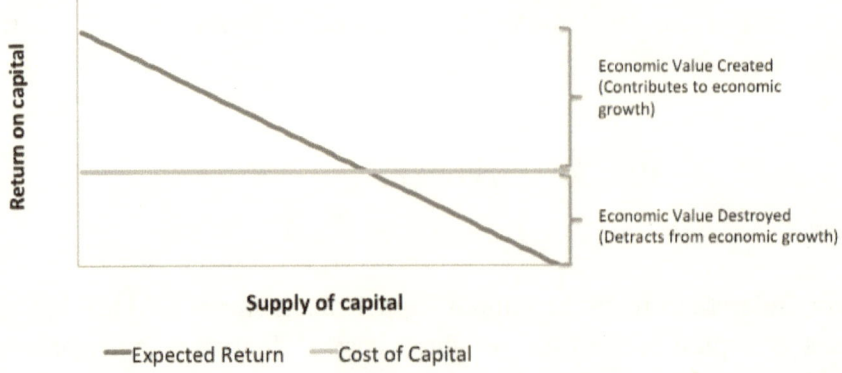

Figure 1: Capital that contributes to economic growth and capital that detracts from economic growth

I suggest that if applied at either a firm level or at a portfolio level of the firms invested in as entrepreneurs in the hope of promoting economic growth, then EVA® will account for the link between the success of entrepreneurs and economic growth and job creation. Thus, entrepreneurs that generate a positive EVA® will contribute to economic growth and those that generate a negative EVA® will destroy economic growth.

This can be seen by looking at both the investment opportunity schedule and the expenditure approach model to GDP.

An increase in EVA® moves the investment opportunity curve to the right and therefore attracts more investment into the portfolio in question. A decrease in EVA® moves the investment opportunity schedule to the left and therefore discourages investment.

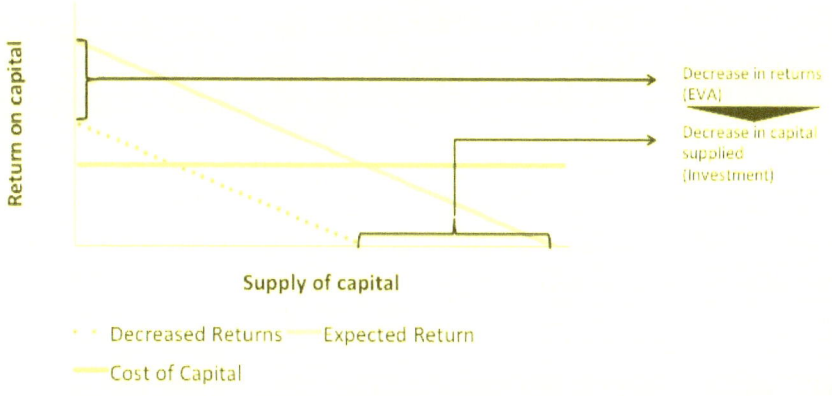

Figure 2: Decreased returns due to subsidies

From the expenditure approach model to GDP:

$$GDP = G + I + (X - M)$$

Any increase in investment will lead to economic growth *ceteris paribus*. Any reduction in investment will decrease economic growth.

Thus, a positive EVA® will attract investment and will generate economic growth, while a negative EVA® will reduce investment and thus detract from economic growth.

Thus, the drivers of EVA ® are important to promoting economic growth and job creation. Most efforts on promoting entrepreneurship focus on the *NOPAT* element of the equation, and these are valid, but the cost of capital is generally neglected.

To be sure, the drivers of *NOPAT* are simplistically: An increase in revenue with a decrease in costs, or at least an appropriate level of control over costs such that total revenues are greater than total costs.

The issue of cost of capital is neglected in the literature as well as in policy and strategies to promote so-called entrepreneurship.

In this book, I argue that at a portfolio level the cost of capital is directly proportionate to the risk of the portfolio. As the number of failures (firms that fail to deliver returns greater than their cost of capital in the long term) in a portfolio of SMMEs/entrepreneurs increase so does the cost of capital of that portfolio. Conversely, as the number of successes increase (firms earning returns greater than their individual cost of capital) so the cost of capital of the portfolio reduces. *Ceteris paribus* as the cost of capital of a portfolio increases, the EVA® for that portfolio decreases, thus decreasing its contribution to economic growth. If the

EVA® of a portfolio is negative, then that portfolio destroys economic value and detracts from economic growth. The reverse is also true.

Increased cost of capital caused by an increase in risk due to an increased failure rate in the national portfolio of SMMEs invested in will decrease the overall investment in that portfolio and therefore in the economy in which that portfolio resides.

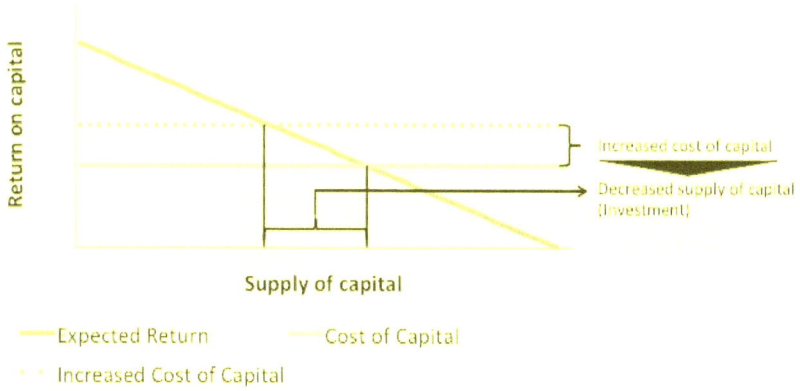

Figure 3: Increased Cost of Capital due to Increased Entrepreneurial Failure at a Portfolio Level

The combined effect thus results in a significant decrease in investment

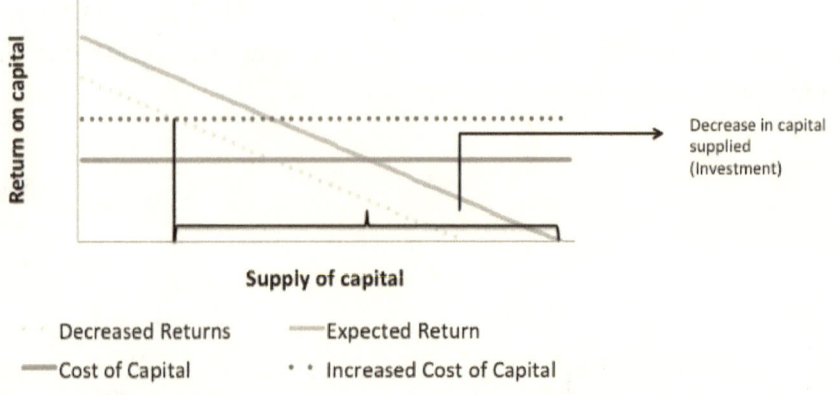

Figure 4: Combined Effects of Increased Cost of Capital & Reduced Returns

As such, at a firm level, we must identify the drivers that:

- Increase revenues
- Decrease costs
- Reduce the risk of failure

Taking the above for granted, at a portfolio level, we must ensure that we reduce the cost of capital for a portfolio.

Our policies, strategies and efforts to drive economic growth and job creation by promoting entrepreneurship must thus focus on increasingly the probability that entrepreneurs will earn a positive EVA®. Thus, our definition of successful entrepreneurship at this stage will be entrepreneurial efforts that generate a positive EVA® within a reasonable period. This reasonable period would be defined by the objectives of the investment. For example, developmental projects that are specifically addressing certain societal issues would certainly accept a longer period before earning a positive EVA® than a purely commercial entrepreneurial investment.

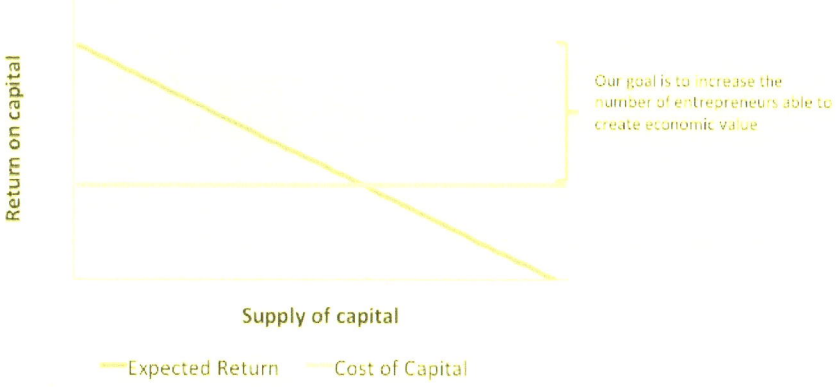

Figure 5: Our focus must be on increasing entrepreneurs that contribute to economic growth by creating economic value

Another way to approach this is as follows:

If we return to our circular-flow model where Gross Domestic Product is equal to the sum of government spending, investment, and exports fewer imports:

$$GDP = C + I + G + (X - M)$$

When a firm reduces the capital stock of the country, it will reduce investments and in the long run, will reduce government spending. Even if it had no impact on government spending, it would still be reducing GDP (and therefore GDP per capita).

The first question is; how does it reduce investment? Very simply, it reduces the capital stock available for investment. This will cause investment to move to more productive markets. If there is only one firm that is earning less than its cost of capital, then the investment will just move to other businesses in the market. If, however, a large section of the economy is earning less than the cost of capital and the remaining section is saturated (supplied with all the capital that it needs) then the investment will move elsewhere, and GDP will shrink.

The second question is; how does it reduce government spending? The reduction in profits will reduce taxes. This will mean that government is earning less and, to continue spending at the same rate (on social grants, infrastructure projects, etc.), will have to borrow money. Unfortunately, it now must pay interest on the borrowed money and, as it borrows more and more (demands more), the price that it must pay for the borrowed money will increase. Thus, in the long run, it will have less to spend and government spending will have to decrease. This will lead to a further increase in the GDP.

The last question is; what about exports? This is an important question that we return to at a later point. For now, it will suffice to say that as the country's economy slows down, it will produce less and will thus be able to export less.

Quite clearly then businesses, and I say businesses rather than entrepreneurs, that do not earn their cost of capital detract from economic growth.

2.2.7 Linking Innovation, Economic Value Added and Economic Growth

The astute reader will now be asking, so where does innovation fit in? This is a very important question, and this is why we spent so much time understanding it. Very simply, we will remember that innovation is the successful commercialisation of a something new, whether it is technology, product, service, idea, or business model. What we did not do was define successful. Success means that the entrepreneur can supply something new to the market in an efficient manner that there is sufficient margin between the price the market is willing to pay and the cost of delivering something new to the market.

We now see that the cost of delivering to the market includes the cost of the capital used in the production of the good or service that is delivered to the market.

So, if we assume that entrepreneurship leads to economic growth, then very simply the entrepreneur must be earning a return equal to or greater than the cost of capital after all costs of production or operation. This is congruent with my suggestion that successful in the context of entrepreneurship, means that the entrepreneurial venture must have a positive EVA®.

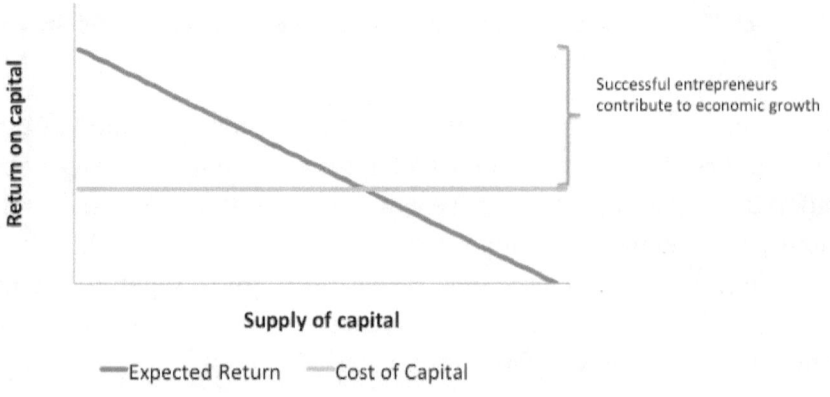

Figure 6: Successful entrepreneurs contribute to economic growth

For entrepreneurship to create jobs, it is not enough for the firm to just grow. If the firm is growing while not earning at least its cost of capital, it will not be sustainable in the long run and the jobs created will be short lived. The firm must grow and create jobs while earning at least its cost of capital.

As a final note, it must be emphasised that in the case where the business is run by the owner or owners (the plural will be used for simplicity) their salaries are not the same as the profit of the firm. The profit is the return on capital, even if the capital belong(s) to the owners. The salaries for running the business must be market-related. If the owners' salaries are paid from the profit, then they are working for free. More accurately, the business is paying their salaries, and the profit is reduced by the value of those salaries. I understand that many small business owners do not draw a salary for tax reasons and I am not going to comment on the legality of this. Even if this is the case, however, the measure of whether the business is successful, is whether its return on capital is at least equal to its cost of capital after accounting for market-related salaries for the owners (if they are active in running or working in the business). If this is not the case, the business is destroying economic value.

2.2.8 Labour

For the purposes of this book, it will be helpful if we understand labour in a very similar way to the way we understand capital. Labour and capital are different, and this must also be understood, but there are parallels, and we will explore these. I must also stress that the term labour is the generic economic term for the product of someone's work, whether that person is the CEO of an organisation or a clerk. Labour, in this context, is not class or role specific.

According to both Adam Smith and Marx, labour or the product of labour is the fundamental unit of value in an economy. Similar to capital, labour commands a return. The difference is that capital demands a return that is related to its risk and commands a return that is a function of how productively the capital is employed. This latter part is similar to labour in that the return commanded by labour is a function of the productivity of that labour. The greater the productivity of labour, the greater the product of that labour and the greater the return that labour will earn.

It is also very important that we understand the distinction between the full return that labour earns and the distribution of that return. Labour is employed by capital (working capital in the form of wages), and typically the capital that employs labour does not belong to the labourer. For this reason, Adam Smith argued that a portion of the return of labour belongs to the labourer and a portion belonged to the owner of the capital that employed the labourer. Karl Marx believed that the full return of labour belongs to the labourer and that none of it belonged to the owner of the capital that employed the labour. The difficulty with Marx's argument, which he recognised, was the fact that this completely removed the incentive for the owner of the capital to use the capital to employ the labour. Marx's solution for this was for the state to own and employ all the capital.

While there are very few today that will agree with Marx's view that the full return of labour belongs to the labourer, the question of distribution continues to be the subject of negotiation to this day. How much of the return of labour belongs to the labourer and how much belongs to the owner of the capital who risks the capital by employing the labour?

What I believe we miss, is the importance of the value of the full return of labour – regardless of whom it belongs to. This does not diminish the importance of fair distribution, but the full return of labour is a precursor to fair distribution. Furthermore, it is critical to our question of economic growth and job creation.

Ultimately, the return of labour contributes to the overall size of the pie that we spoke of at the beginning of this chapter. The greater the return of labour, the greater the contribution of labour to economic growth. Additionally, the greater the return of labour, the greater is the value that can be distributed between the labourer and the owner of the capital that employs the labour. The smaller the return of labour, the more difficult it is to remunerate that labour. Very often the full return of labour is insufficient to provide for the full needs of the labourer providing the labour – without returning a cent to the owner of the capital that employs the labour.

Clearly, the fundamental issue is therefore not the distribution of the return of labour, but the actual size of the return on that labour. The return of labour is neither determined by the owner of the capital who employs the labour nor is it determined by the provider of labour or his or her union. These negotiations revolve around the distribution of the return, but cannot determine the size of the return. The return of labour is determined by the product of that labour which is a function of the productivity of labour. The greater the productivity of labour, therefore, the greater the return on labour. Increasing the productivity of labour is not only central to helping us address the dilemma of remunerating labour fairly, but more importantly in the context of entrepreneurship, it promotes economic growth and sustainable job creation.

What is also important, is that the productivity of labour directly influences how productively our capital is employed. Capital (financial capital) cannot and does not affect the productivity of labour. Thus, by improving the productivity of our labour, we not only earn greater returns on that labour but also earn greater returns on our (financial) capital. Put another way; financial capital cannot be differentiated, it can only be employed more productively. Labour, on the other hand, can be differentiated or improved resulting in greater returns on both the labour and the capital. One of the ways that we improve the productivity of labour is by increasing the human capital of the employed labour. We explore human capital in detail in chapter three. Returning to entrepreneurship and the need to create economic value by earning a return greater than the cost of capital: The productivity of labour increases returns on labour and capital and therefore is critical in our question of creating value. The productivity of labour is thus a critical factor in driving entrepreneurial success that creates economic value.

2.2.9　SMME or Entrepreneur?

Returning to the overall concept of successful entrepreneurship that contributes to economic growth and sustainable job creation: The combination of factors of production in a productive way such that the returns on capital are greater than the cost of capital. This brings me to one of the central assumptions that permeate our current focus on promoting SMMEs. We have assumed that SMMEs are all entrepreneurial, and they might be if you choose a different definition for entrepreneurship. When we want to link entrepreneurship to economic growth and job creation, we can quickly see that an SMME is not automatically entrepreneurial. Many SMMEs might be destroying economic value and detracting from GDP rather than creating economic value and contributing to GDP growth.

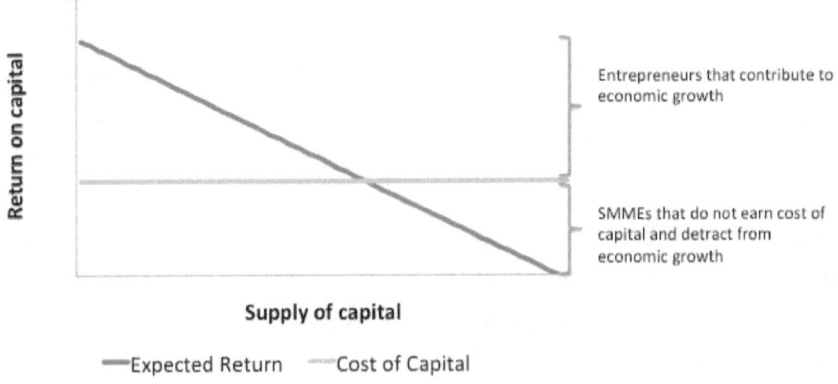

Figure 7: The difference between entrepreneurs and SMMEs

The reader will remember that I highlighted that Schumpeter was talking about big business when he made his argument for innovation-led growth. This was because, he reasoned, these businesses could afford to invest in innovation while still earning their cost of capital. By our definition, however, entrepreneurship is not linked to firm size. It is a function of successful innovation that will lead to the creation of economic value by earning a return on capital greater or equal to the cost of capital. Global research has suggested that firm size is not correlated with job creation and that the optimal firm size differs from country to country.

William Baumol, Robert Litan, Carl Schramm and Robert Strom had this view on this topic in the United States:

"There is much debate and confusion, however, over the definition of the entrepreneur. <u>The outcome matters</u>. Who is given the label <u>frames the way the public and policymakers think about them, and more importantly, their contribution to economic performance</u>." (emphasis added).

For the remainder of the book, entrepreneurs refer to companies that contribute to economic growth and job creation and SMMEs refer to the Small, Medium and Micro Enterprises that do not. I must emphasise again that this construction is one of convenience and is derived from where our focus should be: Addressing unemployment through economic growth and job creation. Entrepreneurs refer to the type of businesses that will contribute to these goals and must, therefore, be the focus of our efforts. I have excluded large businesses, simply because they do not form part of the current focus which targets the SMME sector. The same distinction can (and should) be applied to big businesses. Those that create economic value are entrepreneurial, and those that do not are not entrepreneurial. Most large businesses are public companies and are therefore more directly influenced by market forces that drive them to generate economic profits.

Entrepreneurs, as we have understood them, are important in that they do the following:

- They contribute to economic growth by:

- Earning a return on their capital greater than their cost of capital.
- Increasing the productivity of an economy through innovation.

• Entrepreneurs also contribute to job creation by:
- Growing and;
- Creating new jobs through innovation.

Finally, entrepreneurs help to balance the labour market when jobs are lost in one area and created in another.

3 Chapter Three: What are the Drivers of "Entrepreneurial Success"?

Having understood what entrepreneurial success looks like if we want to promote economic growth and job creation, we must now understand what the drivers of this success are. This will enable us to understand what to look for when developing a strategy for promoting this type of entrepreneurship.

Of strategy, Joan Magretta of the Institute for Strategy and Competitiveness at Harvard Business School once said: *"Of all the concepts in management, strategy is one that attracts the most attention and generates the most controversy. Almost everyone agrees that it's important. Almost no one agrees on what it is."* As we have seen, this statement is equally true in the concept of entrepreneurs. It is even more so when it comes to understanding what drives entrepreneurial success.

As with any of the social sciences, we must understand at the outset that entrepreneurship is not an exact science and that even the most widely accepted theories are criticised and limited in their application. Entrepreneurship exists in the highly subjective and complex world where no two scenarios are ever replicable, many of the causal variables are undoubtedly overlooked, and anyone who attempts to reduce entrepreneurship to an exact, replicable science robs it of its essence.

Murray Low and Ian Macmillan of the University of Pennsylvania, remind us that entrepreneurship is a highly complex process with innumerable interactions between the entrepreneur and the environment and an indefinite number of stakeholders thus making it incredibly difficult to develop replicable algorithms for identifying potentially successful entrepreneurs.

With this in mind, there are several enablers and inhibitors that have been identified, and there are sufficient evidence and consensus to warrant discussion.

Broadly, the drivers of entrepreneurial success are financial capital and human capital. Remember that an entrepreneur combines factors of production in pursuit of profit. These factors are (financial) capital and labour. Human capital plays a vital role in two ways: Firstly, it increases the productivity of labour. Secondly, the entrepreneur's human capital makes the entrepreneur more productive when combining other factors of production. Specifically, it is the very nature of this highly complex process with innumerable interactions between the entrepreneur and the environment and an indefinite number of stakeholders that calls for a very specific type and quality of human capital. We discuss each of these in detail below.

3.1 Financial Capital

It is unlikely that the reader is unfamiliar with the notion that a lack of access to finance is a major barrier to many would-be entrepreneurs and entrepreneurs. This assumption is taken for granted in most of the academic and policymaking discussion in South Africa. Unfortunately, very little empirical testing has been done, and the little which has been done is largely based on survey data, which are subjective. Fortunately, as we will see, there is sufficient evidence to support this notion. I believe that the research and policy discussion falls short in identifying the root cause of why would-be entrepreneurs and entrepreneurs battle to secure financing. I attempt to address this later by using what available objective empirical evidence exists in conjunction with solid economic theory. Before we address why access to financial capital is a challenge, we will explore financial capital as an enabler of entrepreneurial success.

Perhaps one of the reasons that this is taken as self-evident (and at the same time, why breakthrough research findings that declare that access to finance is a barrier to entrepreneurship, is so underwhelming) is simply that it is self-evident by construction.

Returning to our conglomerate of definitions, an entrepreneur is someone who employs (financial) capital to earn a return. Almost implicitly, the entrepreneur has a need for capital – otherwise, why would they undertake the entrepreneurial risk? Adam Smith and ensuing economists up to Schumpeter combined the capitalist (owner and provider of capital) and the entrepreneur, suggesting that the entrepreneur had sufficient capital of their own. This might sometimes be the case, but based on the mere existence of the various types of formalised financing – angel investors, venture capitalists, private equity firms, banks, bond markets and securities exchanges, we can safely assume that this is not always the case. Furthermore, Adam Smith emphasised in his work that interest rates were correlated with profits as the profit had to be sufficient to pay the interest as well as provide a return to the entrepreneur. This implies that the entrepreneur was borrowing money (financial capital) to fund his venture. Furthermore, both Cantillon and Schumpeter emphasised that the entrepreneur was supplied with financial capital by the investor (the owner of capital). By implication, the entrepreneur did not possess the required capital to pursue their entrepreneurial efforts. This is the self-evident or *a priori* reasoning. It makes sense.

The reader willing to accept this is welcome to skip to the next section, but for those who want to explore the empirical evidence, the following briefly explores the evidence. The summary of the following section (for those willing to accept it) is that:

- Start-ups battle more than anyone to secure financing.
- Small firms battle to find funding.
- As firm size increases, access to finance becomes easier.
- Access to finance is an enabler of growth for the firm.

In the following section, I have reverted to academic referencing convention so that the reader can follow the references.

3.1.1 An academic review of financial capital and entrepreneurial success

After an extensive review of 119 influential academic articles on this subject, the following emerged:

To begin with, the widely used model of *Entrepreneurial choice under liquidity constraints* (Evans & Jovanovic, 1989) concludes that liquidity constraints bind and that entrepreneurs are constrained by access to finance. Even in the re-estimation of this model (Xu, 1998) and in the dynamic model developed to answer questions about the validity of the Evans-Jovanovic static model (Buera, 2009); the underlying assumptions are that there is pre-venturing wealth accumulation (savings) to enable successful venturing. This strongly suggests that access to finance (of some sort – in this case savings) is necessary for successful venturing.

Work by Beck, Demirgüç-Kunt, & Maksimovic (2005) that uses survey data to assess relationships between the financing obstacles that firms report and actual firm growth finds that the negative impact of reported obstacles such as access to finance, on firm growth, is stronger for small firms than large firms, but present in both cases. This work has the advantage of using cross-country, firm-level data, but the disadvantage of relying on survey responses. To address this weakness, a different methodology is used by Beck, Demirguc-Kunt, Laeven, & Levine (2008) to assess the growth of small firms in countries with better developed financial systems. This work provides complementary information to that of Beck, Demirgüç-Kunt, & Maksimovic (2005), showing that small firms do indeed grow faster with better access to finance.

When looking at the impact of access to finance on start-ups, further robust evidence suggests that access to finance is particularly important to both small (Beck et al., 2008; Beck, Demirgüç-Kunt, Laeven, & Levine, 2004) and new (Beck, Demirgüç-Kunt, Laeven, & Maksimovic, 2006) businesses. When adjusting the definition of a small enterprise down and using four cut-offs namely; 100, 50, 10 and five employees, Beck et al. demonstrate evidence that small firms are significantly more constrained by lack of access to finance (Beck et al., 2008).

Beck & Demirgüc-Kunt (2006) also provide empirical evidence to suggest a causal relationship between access to finance and growth, answering the question of whether obstacles to accessing finance inhibit growth. Their evidence strongly suggests that obstacles to securing finance, hinders growth and they find this increasingly so, as the size of the firm becomes smaller. What they do not explore is whether the obstacles to accessing finance (such as a paucity of human capital) are in themselves causal in hindering growth, or whether it is purely the absence of finance that hinders the growth. This is an important consideration when considering the interplay between human capital and both access to and the application of financial capital, which we will explore later. We do see, however, that firms that require external funding (regardless of size) grow faster when such funding is available (Beck, Demirgüç-Kunt, & Maksimovic, 2005; Demirgüç-Kunt & Maksimovic, 1998; Zingales, Fama, Klenow, & Rodriguez-clare, 1996).

Furthermore, two influential papers support the views that access to finance is critical for new firms (start-ups) (Cetorelli & Strahan, 2013) and for the growth of smaller firms (Guiso, Sapienza, & Zingales, 2004). It is interesting that when differentiating between size and age, size is more important in developing economies and age in developed economies (Beck et al., 2006). What is problematic with each of these approaches is that their studies investigate existing firms, thus assuming success at least to a certain degree. The absence of failing firms in the data used by these papers again fails to answer the "why" regarding the difficulties small firms face around accessing capital. At the very least, the underlying assumption in these pieces is that otherwise would-be successful entrepreneurs can be more successful when supplied with the necessary capital – *ceteris paribus*. **The findings in these papers do not suggest that by making finance easily accessible, we will make firms that would otherwise not have been successful, successful**.

We also see a discussion around smaller firms being more financially constrained (Devereux & Schiantarelli, 1990; Oliner & Rudebusch, 1992) and that as far as perception goes, small firms perceive higher financing obstacles than large ones (Schiffer & Weder, 2001), as well as being more constrained in their operational growth (Berger & Udell, 1998; Galindo & Schiantarelli, 2003). Yet again, an important question that is not answered is: Why? One of the reasons for this is that the smaller firms not only have a higher cost of capital and are less likely to earn their cost of capital and are therefore less likely to be able to access funding.

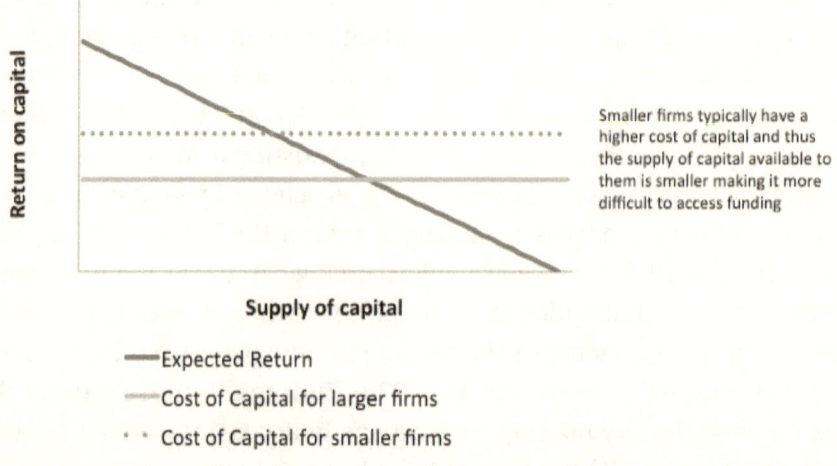

Figure 8: Cost of Capital typically increases as firm size decreases

Importantly Zingales et al. (1996) confirm in their influential work that in general, on a macroeconomic scale, accessible finance for firms leads to growth. Furthermore, a revisit of the work by Fisman & Love (2007) confirms that accessible finance leads not only to firm growth but also economic growth. This is to be expected in the light of the expenditure approach to GDP, which we have already discussed in detail:

$$GDP = C + I + G + (X - M)$$

Counter arguments include those that point to human capital, rather than financial capital to be a determinant of success (Cressy, 1996). This is probably because the absence of human capital decreases access to and application of financial capital (Pissarides, 1999a) by increasing the risk of the investment. That is: *Access to finance is likely to be lower in the absence of human capital and the application of available financial capital in the absence of human capital is also probably less likely to lead to success.* We can see for example that Business Development Services (an investment that develops human capital) does increase access to free market financial capital (Mazanai & Fatoki, 2011), suggesting that Business Development Services (BDS) reduce the risk of the investment or at the very least, the perceived risk. Similarly, we see that entrepreneurial orientation affects access to financial capital (Fatoki, 2012). What is clear in all the counter-arguments is that there is no disproof of the importance of access to finance, but rather the argument that there are in fact, intervening variables – particularly appropriate human capital. This is an important consideration that highlights the need for establishing the reasons behind why access to finance might be a problem. It is important to emphasise again, that implicit in all the literature that access to finance promotes firm growth and even economic growth. This is the premise that the market assigns this finance to firms that are likely to earn a return equal to or greater than their cost of capital. For whatever reasons, it is implicit that financial capital is supplied where the probability of success already exists.

Briefly: In the South African context, much of the literature on constraints to entrepreneurship in South Africa cite lack of access to finance as a major constraint, although generally either just accepting it as an assumption or using perception based survey-level data. For example (Fatoki, 2012; Herrington, Kew, Simrie, & Turton, 2011; Ligthelm, 2010; Mbonyane & Ladzani, 2011; Mbonyane, 2006; Mthente Research and Consulting Services (Pty) Ltd, 2012; Rogerson, 2008; Rolfe, Woodward, Ligthelm, & Guimarães, 2010; Schoombee, 2000b, 1999a, 2000a; Stander, 2011), with one exception (Callaghan, 2012), no empirical evidence comparable to the rigor used by Beck et al. could be found in the South African literature. Since there is empirical evidence to support these claims and since Beck et al. include South Africa in their cross-country data, one might assume that it is a reasonable assumption that these data hold for South Africa. Thus, the assumption is that the preceding discussions are applicable in the South African context, given the same implicit assumptions already identified: That the data assumes that finance is supplied at a market-related cost of capital and assumes a reasonable probability of a positive return.

In summary, it is reasonable to accept that financial capital is an enabler of success. While it is apparent that access to finance is *inter alia* a function of human capital and that the successful application of financial capital is also dependent, at least to a degree, on the level of human capital, financial capital is a critical enabler of success in its own right, without which human capital would be insufficient to enable successful entrepreneurship.

3.2 Human Capital

I start off by differentiating between human capital and entrepreneurial capital and by emphasising that both are concepts that are still being discussed and debated by both academics and practitioners. Since I am working conceptually, I have elected to use the concept of human capital rather than entrepreneurial capital. This is because the concept of human capital is better developed than that of entrepreneurial capital. This is also because the concept of entrepreneurial capital includes human capital which is appropriate to the entrepreneurial venture. As such, when I talk about human capital, I specifically mean human capital which is appropriate to the entrepreneurial venture. I will discuss this appropriateness in more detail, but for now, I will give a simple example. Computer programming knowledge, skills, experience and qualifications will all fall under the concept of human capital. This human capital will be extremely appropriate for an entrepreneur starting an IT business. It will be almost meaningless for an entrepreneur starting a plumbing business. Thus, the appropriateness is context specific.

According to Prof Truls Erikson's paper, published through the Manchester Business School, entrepreneurial capital is a "heterogeneous resource, consisting of a set of complementary human capacities." These include entrepreneurial commitment and entrepreneurial competence or appropriate human capital.

Human capital is the total collection of skills, knowledge and personal attributes that collectively give the ability to produce economic value. We briefly explore human capital from an academic point of view. After this, we will discuss it more plainly in the context of enabling entrepreneurial success.

The concept of human capital was introduced by Nobel Laureate, Prof Theodore Schultz of The University of Chicago and developed by another Nobel Laureate of The University of Chicago, Prof Gary Becker. Based on Schultz's argument that knowledge and skills are factors of production that can be gained, it is implicit that human capital can be added to, through education and experience.

Broadly, we would accept *a priori* that human capital is positively associated with entrepreneurial success especially since the ability to produce economic value is endogenous to our definition of human capital. Human capital is widely seen as both an enabler of entrepreneurial success and a driver of performance. Some authors have gone so far as to suggest that it can be a substitute for financial capital to a reasonable degree, but more importantly, in my opinion, a mitigator of financial risk. Furthermore, we see that human capital is an antecedent not only for firm growth but also for economic growth. Both Schultz and Becker show that higher levels of human capital result in greater productivity of both labour and capital.

Included under human capital are the concepts of skills, knowledge, experience and education. Education is typically a means of gaining knowledge and skills. Experience represents the application of the knowledge and development of skills. Thus, education and experience are proxies for knowledge and skills. Since it is knowledge and skills that are critical, I will refer to these, but I do use the proxies of education and experience where appropriate.

To understand how these, influence entrepreneurial success, I break them down into two broad domains.

The first of these is the set of knowledge and skills particular to the actual product or service. For a dentist, these would be the knowledge gained in medical school, the experience gained during an internship and through practice. Similarly, for a pilot, knowledge and skills are gained during flight training and through years of experience. These are specific to the type of entrepreneurial venture, and I refer to these as technical skills, experience, education or knowledge. These skills are typically employed as a factor of production, namely labour. They are the skills that are combined with other factors of production in the delivery of a product or service.

The second set of skills are those skills needed to successfully commercialise the technical skills. These might often be referred to as business acumen. The subjects covered in business school would give a good representation of these:

- Strategy
- Marketing
- Sales
- Finance
- Accounting
- Economics
- Operations Management
- People Management
- Leadership

The items on this list are neither mutually exclusive nor collectively exhaustive, but they give an idea of the skills set required to run a business. I refer to these as commercial skills, experience, education or knowledge. These form the part of the human capital that is used to combine the other factors of production including labour (typically the technical skills) in delivering the products or services. This is why the commercial skills are sometimes differentiated into a sub-set of human capital known as entrepreneurial capital since it is the entrepreneur who combines other factors of production (including the human capital which is used by labour) in pursuit of profit. We have already noted that the distinction between entrepreneurial capital and human capital is not perfect. For example, commercial skills can be employed in the form of managers who employ these skills to manage the enterprise. It is important to understand that we are dealing with concepts and that the precise demarcations of our definitions are blurry.

The technical set of skills are vital in terms of the actual production or delivery of the product or service, and this should be self-evident. Don't try and develop a software package if you don't know how to turn on a computer. From an entrepreneurial point of view, the commercial set of skills is equally critical. It is difficult to emphasise one over the other. Both need to exist in every business.

In South Africa and across Africa, the lack of human capital is a widely recognised problem among SMMEs, although any level of specificity beyond human capital is just as scarce in the academic literature. We need to understand why this lack of human capital is fundamental to our problem of economic growth and job creation.

One of the (few) most important empirical findings in the South African academic literature is that human capital increases access to financial capital.

Why is this? While the answer is intuitively self-evident, we find that when we answer this question in detail, we also find the answer to an earlier asked question. The reader will remember that I emphasised that there was no breakthrough in the finding that access to funding is a barrier to entrepreneurs. The more prominent issue is to find out why would-be entrepreneurs struggle to find funding.

Before going further, I must now refine my own definition of human capital. Human capital for entrepreneurial success is the appropriate mix of technical and commercial skills, knowledge, experience and education for the entrepreneurial venture in question. From here on, this is what I am referring to when I speak of human capital, whether the entrepreneur possesses all of these (which is extremely unlikely) or they are possessed collectively by the owner(s) and the staff that are employed.

This human capital increases the productivity of the entrepreneurial venture, as well as the likelihood of successful innovation that would lead to commercial success. Thus, the human decreases the risk associated with the entrepreneurial venture. It shouldn't be difficult to see this, but let me ask the reader to bet on the success of two entrepreneurs, both of whom have decided to start an IT business. The first grew up in a rural area, didn't complete matric, did a short course in computer programming and spent five years working as a low-level technician for a small software company that eventually went bankrupt. The second not only finished school and earned a Masters' Degree in IT through Stanford (the same university that the founders of Google went to), but also completed an MBA through Harvard after completing three years as a software engineer for Google. Both need $1 million for their IT start-up. The education and work experience are proxies for skills and experience but the statistical chances of success for the second entrepreneur are significantly higher than those for the first. Why? We assume (quite confidently) that the second has both significantly better technical and commercial skills than the first.

Intuitively we know that the second would-be entrepreneur is more likely to get financing and be successful. The technical reason for this is that the increased human capital will almost certainly lead to higher levels of productivity and innovation. This increases the chance of success, lowering the risk and in turn, the cost of capital is lowered. Combined with the increase in chances of success the probability that the returns will equal or exceed the cost of capital, increases. This easily helps us to understand how the market allocates capital to entrepreneurship, but it is important for us to understand why this is so important.

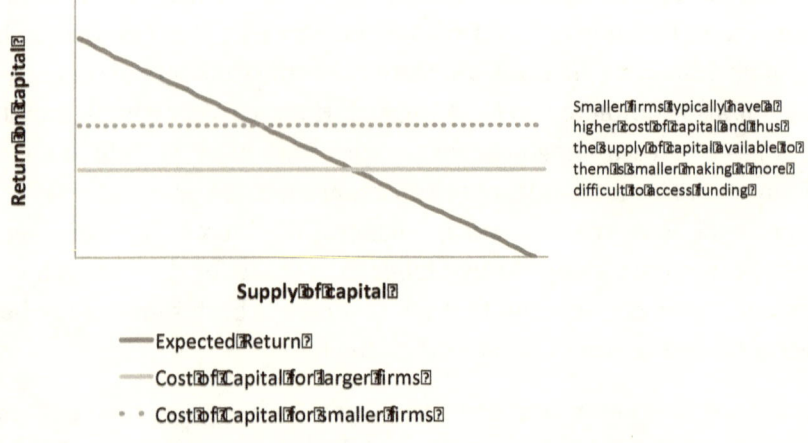

Figure 9: Smaller firms experience greater difficulty in accessing finance due to a higher cost of capital

4 Chapter Four: Why is our current strategy for promoting SMMEs flawed?

4.1 The importance of free market allocation of capital

The first key issue that we must understand is that while capital is finite, that there isn't a shortage. We know this because capital is both available and affordable in many instances. A shortage would artificially drive up the price. Thus, we know that the cost of capital is driven primarily by risk rather than by supply and demand. If anything, with low-interest rates around the world the capital market is possibly oversupplied rather than undersupplied.

The next key issue we must understand is that when capital is poorly allocated, and the cost of allocated capital exceeds the return on that capital, economic value is destroyed. It is, therefore, important that capital is appropriately allocated to ensure both economic growth and job creation.

In a free market, suppliers of capital are looking to maximise the returns on their investment relative to the risk. They are not looking to only cover their cost of capital, they are looking to receive a return that is as high above their cost of capital as possible. They are therefore seeking out opportunities to either lend or invest their capital in entrepreneurs that will give them a return greater than the cost of capital. If a would-be entrepreneur is unable to secure financing, it is very likely that the investors believe that the returns will not exceed the cost of capital.

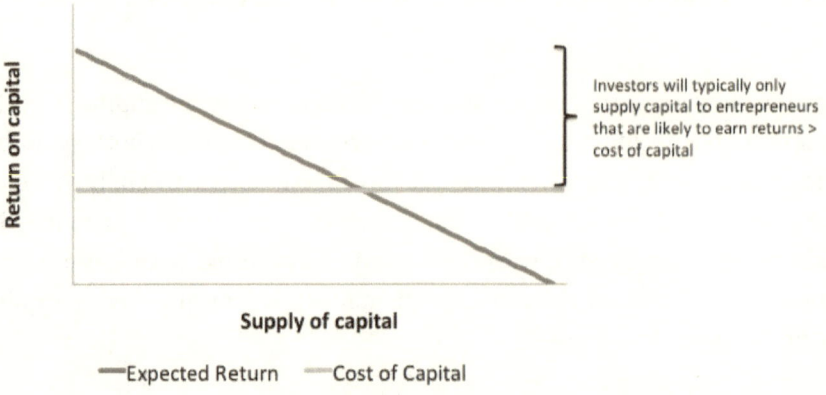

Figure 10: Free market funding will typically find its way to entrepreneurs that are likely to deliver returns greater than Cost of Capital

Typically, the risk involved in entrepreneurship is already high - highest at the start-up phase and gradually lowering as the business matures. This means that the cost of capital is correspondingly high. The human capital and the quality of the commercial proposition are the means that the suppliers of capital use to estimate the risk, the associated cost of capital and the potential returns. Where the suppliers of capital believe that there is a reasonable possibility of earning a positive return on their capital, they will supply capital. In doing so and if this return materialises, they are contributing to economic growth and job creation. We have already seen that by allocating capital to ventures that were high-risk and provided a return below the cost of capital or went bankrupt, they are destroying economic value.

It is thus imperative that capital is allocated in such a manner that the aggregate return on the invested capital of the economy is greater than the aggregate cost of this capital.

I have the unenviable task of concluding that if would-be entrepreneurs are battling to secure financing, it is because the entrepreneurial opportunity they are pursuing does not show enough promise of earning a return greater than the cost of capital. I would suggest, based on academic literature, the little empirical evidence that exists and my own experience, that on aggregate the primary reason for this is the absence to a greater or lesser degree of human capital.

Thus, the market is doing exactly what is predicted.

We now know where we are – which intuitively we already knew, but more importantly, we have a better understanding of why. The next important questions are:

- Do we want to change this?
- Why do we want to change this?

- What is the best way to change this?

The first two questions are easy to answer. The answer to the first is yes, but leads to another question. What exactly do we want to change? I believe that this is where we have gone wrong. The answer to why helps to understand what we want to change and how we can find the best way of changing it.

Our fundamental goal is economic growth and job creation, not the promotion of SMMEs. We want to change the current situation because we want to promote entrepreneurship that promotes economic growth and sustainable job creation.

This inadvertently answers what we want to change and this is critical: We want to increase the supply of entrepreneurship (as we have now understood it) demanding capital. This also tells us what we do not want to do: We do not want to increase the supply of capital to businesses that are going to destroy economic value. Unfortunately, this is exactly what we are doing.

How are we increasing the supply of capital to businesses that destroy economic value? We are doing this by making more money available through various funds and departments of government to specifically target SMMEs that cannot secure funding based on merit, or by reducing the price that the consumer of the capital (would-be entrepreneur) pays for it (interest).

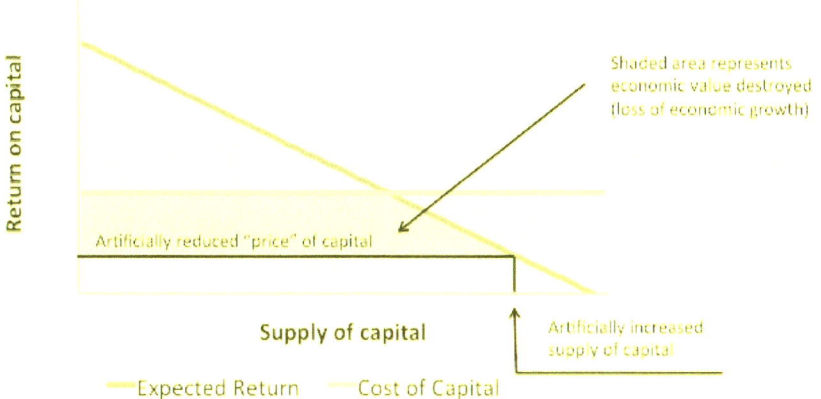

Figure 11: Economic value destroyed by artificially increasing the supply of capital

There are several problems with this approach, and we will explore them in detail.

4.2 WHAT IS WRONG WITH INCREASING THE SUPPLY OF FINANCIAL CAPITAL?

4.2.1 Cost of Capital and negative EVA ®

We have seen that one of the ways to increase the supply of capital is to reduce the price of the capital. Firstly, I deliberately say price and not cost, for reasons that I will explain shortly, but before I do this, we must understand the price of capital in the context that I use it.

Capital belongs to the supplier of capital who expects a return for the use of the capital. This will depend on how the capital is supplied. When funding a business, there are two main ways that this capital is supplied in a competitive market. The one is debt financing, and the other is equity financing. Both should be familiar to the reader.

In debt financing, the entrepreneur applies for a loan and must repay the loan with interest over a period of time. The interest is the price that the entrepreneur pays for the use of the capital.

In equity financing, the supplier of capital purchases a share in the entrepreneur's business. This share commands a portion of the company's profit. This share of profit or dividends is the price of the capital. Obviously, the percentage share that the supplier of the capital purchases, is a function of both the value of the capital supplied and the expected future profits of the business. Simplistically, the cost of capital would determine the investor's expected return. The annual profits would be estimated, and this would be used to determine what share of the profit would meet the expected return on the total capital supplied.

The third type of financing occurs in markets where there is an intervention (typically by the government), and this is known as grant financing. This type of financing is donated, and no price is paid for the capital.

The price can thus be lowered by determining a lower interest rate than the risk would demand, taking a smaller share than the capital would command in a free market or by giving grant financing.

The problem is that price of capital does not lower the cost of capital any more than subsiding the price of any product or service lowers the cost of bringing that product or service to the market. This tells us that where the price is subsidised, the cost is borne somewhere else. If the price is subsidised by the government, the cost is borne by the taxpayers. This would be acceptable if the total gain to the economy were greater than the cost. Unfortunately, it is not. The reason for this is simple - the subsidy is needed to provide financing to would-be entrepreneurs who would not be able to access capital in a free market. They cannot access the funds because the risk involved in investing in their business makes the cost of capital prohibitive. As we have seen, by making this capital more affordable by lowering the price, we do not lower the cost. We now end up providing capital to businesses that are not able to earn the cost of that capital. As a consequence, we end up funding businesses that are destroying, rather than creating economic value and detracting from GDP growth rather than contributing to it. This has the knock-on effect of destroying jobs, not creating them.

4.2.2   Increasing the supply of businesses that destroy economic value

By artificially increasing the supply of capital, we increase the demand for that capital. Thus, we succeed in increasing the number of businesses that demand capital at a price lower than their cost of capital. While we may pat ourselves on the back for increasing the number of businesses (most often SMMEs) in the economy, we have increased the number of businesses that are destroying economic value.

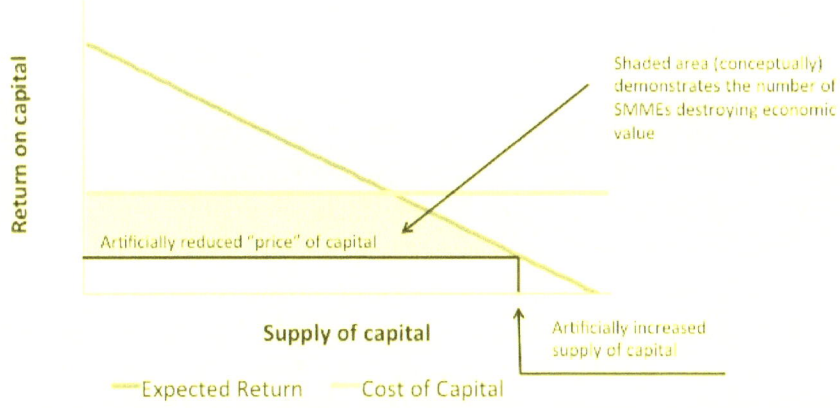

Figure 12: Artificially increased supply of capital increases number of SMMEs destroying economic value

4.2.3 Entrepreneurial agency theory

Entrepreneurial agency theory is a theory that I have adapted from the agency developed by Prof Michael Jensen of Harvard University. Agency theory addresses the agency problem of incentivising directors (agents) to act in the interests of shareholders (principals). One of Jensen's solutions is for the company to borrow against future earnings and pay the cash out to shareholders in dividends, thus sucking all the profit out of the business and forcing the directors to be thrifty and efficient in the running of the business to meet their debt obligations.

A similar concept can apply to entrepreneurship. The entrepreneur, faced with the risk of bankruptcy due to the cost of servicing debt, will be incentivised to make their business as efficient as possible to avoid defaulting on their debt obligations. The subsidy of financial capital to any degree reduces this incentive. Consequently, the entrepreneur might be less inclined to maximise the efficiencies within their business. This lack of efficiency at the very least reduces their contribution to economic growth. I must include the *caveat* that this remains a theory. I have, in my research, tested this through a few qualitative methods including, but not limited to interviews with Professors of Economics as well as practitioners. While the interviews offered structure to this theory, I have no empirical evidence to support it. I submit to the readership of this book that is nothing more than a well-developed and effectively untested theory.

4.2.4 Unhealthy competition by exceeding market supply equilibrium: Promoting too Many Businesses and Destroying Entrepreneurship

We know from economic theory that every market has a certain carrying capacity. If there is an oversupply in any given market, competition will rise to a point where a few incumbents exit the market either voluntarily through diversification or involuntarily by liquidation. In a free market system, this competition ensures that only the most innovative and most efficient survive and free markets are thus more or less self-regulating. Simplistically, in a free market that is free of subsidy and monopoly, the market demand will not only regulate price levels, but it will regulate the number of competitors that a market can support.

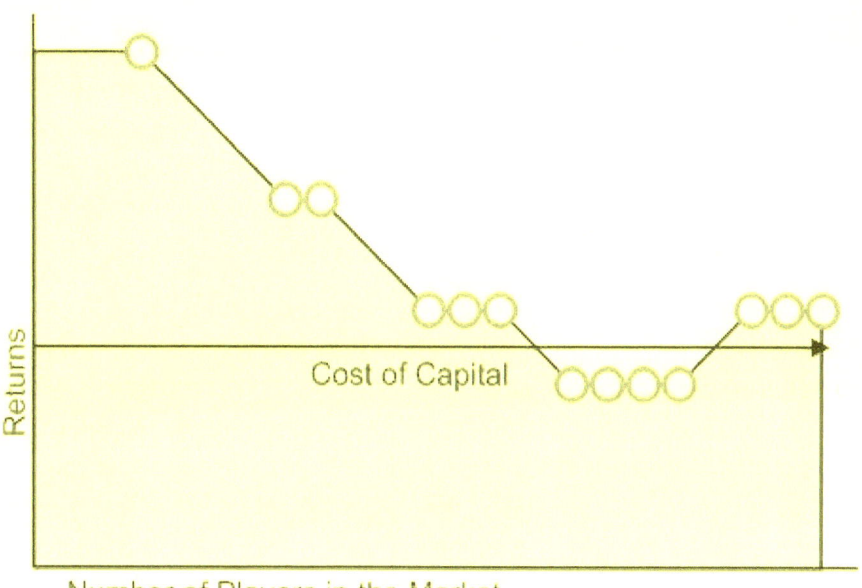

Figure 13: Market Equilibrium

Promotion of too many businesses increases competition beyond the normal free market limit, thus reducing margins are reducing economic value added of all incumbents.

The reduced margin not only erodes the creation of economic value, but limits resources available for innovation as all incumbents are fighting for survival. It must be remembered that Schumpeter specifically noted that businesses that could afford to invest in innovation were those most likely to drive economic growth. Schumpeter implicitly argued that businesses needed sufficient margin to invest in innovation that would drive economic growth. By eroding these margins through artificially maintaining too many competitors, we are reducing the ability of entrepreneurs to invest in innovation.

If we consider the example of a small village and its need for a doctor, it is quite plausible to suggest that the village will quite possibly have a need for no more than one doctor, perhaps two on the outside. If a third doctor opens a practice, there will not be enough patients to support all the doctors. Eventually one of them will decide that there is simply not enough business and will close his or her practice. If, however, the new doctor is paid by the government, he or she will be sufficiently remunerated regardless of the number of patients their practice sees. Even without undercutting the other doctors this new doctor will reduce their market share to the point where one eventually goes out of business. If this doctor can undercut the other doctors, this will put one or both out of business even sooner.

It is unlikely that the doctor subsidised by the government will undercut the other two because there is no motivation to do so. The subsidised doctor receives no extra money for seeing additional patients and will only increase his or her workload by undercutting the other two. It is more likely that this subsidised doctor would prefer to operate inefficiently and not undercut the other two.

Let us consider the example of a state-owned airline that is competing with private airlines. The airline industry has very small margins, and it is extremely difficult to make a profit. Airline travel is also not easy to differentiate and so, one of the few ways to compete is on price. The private airlines will be forced to do so, but the government airline will not since their business is subsidised. The government airline will operate less efficiently than its private counterparts and in doing so, will destroy economic value by not making the most productive use of its capital. In addition to this, it will reduce the ability of the private airlines who do make productive use of their capital to generate less economic value than they should. Thus, the government airline not only destroys value in its own business but forces others – who would otherwise be creating value – to destroy value as well. This is an altogether pernicious situation.

The same applies to subsidised businesses. Firstly, it is likely that they are destroying economic value themselves, both through their own inefficiency which would have prevented them from securing financing in the first place and by providing a return on their capital that is lower than the cost of capital. Secondly, they are crowding the true entrepreneurs who would have created value or at the very least, reducing the amount of value they can create. Finally, as we have seen, these subsidised businesses erode margins and reduce the investment that entrepreneurs can make in future innovations. Subsidised entrepreneurship is simply an extension of government, which is inherently inefficient all over the world, competing with the private sector.

4.2.5 Crowding out free market investors

In the same way that subsidised businesses crowd out entrepreneurs, subsidised capital crowds out investors. Investors make their living by earning a return on their capital that they allow others to use in pursuit of their entrepreneurial ventures. In doing so, we have seen that they play a crucial role in creating economic value. Not only do they increase the capital stock of the economy by earning returns greater than their cost of capital, but they enable entrepreneurs to do so as well. In the process of doing so, the entrepreneurs increase the productivity of the economy, thereby increasing the purchasing power of society and increasing its wealth. By reducing the market share of entrepreneurs by increasing the number of less efficient businesses, the entrepreneurs can only offer smaller returns to their investors. This has the effect of reducing the total volume of free market investment available in the economy, and we know that when investment is reduced, economic growth is reduced.

Even if we could replace all the private investment with government investment, the result would still be undesirable. The reason for this is that private suppliers of capital are more efficient at supplying capital than governments. The reason for this is obvious - this is their business, this is how they earn a living. In addition to this, they are often investing their own money and share in the entrepreneurial risk. They are more likely to supply capital to entrepreneurs that will create substantial economic value and many jobs.

There are other undesirable consequences of crowding out the private suppliers of capital. Several these investors supply more than just financial capital. Very often, they bring years of experience to the businesses that they are investing in and in doing so, they are helping to augment the human capital in the businesses that they are investing in. Over and above this, they often have strong networks that the entrepreneurs they are investing in can leverage to grow their business. This is all in the investors' interests because, as we have seen, they often stand to lose as much, if not more than the entrepreneur if the venture is unsuccessful.

Finally, having invested in a business, investors have established a relationship with a business. This will help to reduce the asymmetry of information and will assist the entrepreneur in accessing capital for expansion at a later stage.

4.3 CONCLUSION

It is very clear that increasing the supply of capital to businesses to increase the number of SMMEs, will probably achieve this goal and in doing so, actively destroy economic growth. It will also destroy jobs. This might be counter-intuitive since a few the SMMEs will create jobs. The problem is that they will create fewer jobs than truly entrepreneurial companies would and they will also destroy many jobs by unfairly competing with their entrepreneurial counterparts. The net result will be fewer jobs in the economy.

From this, it follows that we are achieving exactly the opposite of what we want. Rather than contributing to economic growth and creating jobs, we are reducing economic growth and destroying jobs.

5 Chapter Five: Developing a Solution

As stated, to achieve our joint goals of economic growth and job creation we need to increase the number of entrepreneurs rather than the number of SMMEs.

What we haven't done is explicitly answer the question of how to do this.

The evidence points overwhelmingly in the direction of addressing the human capital needed for entrepreneurship. This solution is problematic in an economy where the education system is largely broken. It is neither an easy nor a quick fix. We will address the need for developing human capital in more detail. It is not new to say that we need to improve the level of skills in the country. The question that hasn't been answered is: Which skills? Notwithstanding, I will make a bold statement: If we were to completely leave entrepreneurship alone and focus all our efforts on properly addressing not only the shortage of skills but also the shortage of quality skills, then the problem of entrepreneurship would fix itself. To be clear, I'm not saying that the lack of quality skills is our only problem. There are other problems, but if we had to choose just one thing to focus all of our energy on, then I would suggest that we could pick a bigger problem to solve.

Returning to the issue of which skills and remembering that in this book I am speaking specifically about entrepreneurship: The reader will remember that the first set of skills are what I referred to as technical skills. The big question here is which technical skills? Do we promote developing the skills of doctors, or lawyers, or engineers, or artisans or farmers? I will not provide a list of skills, but I will rather discuss how these skills should be identified. The short answer is that we need to decide which areas we want to promote entrepreneurship in. Which areas does our country have a potential competitive advantage? Which areas hold the most promise for contributing to economic growth and job creation? We need to identify these areas and then focus on developing technical skills in these areas. We will return to the question of which technical skills after looking at the simpler, more generic, second set of skills.

5.1 Developing commercial skills: A multidisciplinary set of skills required combine factors of production in a way that reduces risk and maximises value creation.

The second set of skills is commercial skills. Fortunately, these are more generic or less industry specific. Our country and our continent have a massive shortage of quality skills needed to effectively run a business. Even highly qualified individuals with strong technical skills are often terrible at running a business. This is neither uncommon nor is it wrong. Technical specialists are specialists by nature, whereas business skills are more general. Technical specialists should not, in an ideal world, try to focus on running a business. They should rather focus on what they are good at and partner with someone that is more commercially skilled. The problem is that there are very few appropriately qualified or experienced business people that they can either partner with or employ.

I also deliberately mention quality as this is a major shortcoming of ours, both in South Africa and in Africa. To be sure, there are some outstanding business qualifications. The University of Cape Town offers an MBA that is, at the time of writing, ranked as the 52nd best in the world[3]. That is massively impressive considering that there are over 70 000 business schools in the world. Sadly, it is the only business school in Africa that ranks in the top 100 MBAs globally. There are only three[4] other business schools that have triple international accreditation: The University of Stellenbosch, Henley Business School and the University of Cairo. Of these three, only the University of Stellenbosch and the University of Cairo have achieved 5 palms[4] status. Unfortunately, there are several MBAs in the country that are of questionable quality. That is to say nothing of the lower business qualifications, many of which provide a would-be entrepreneur or manager with very little to no value with

---

[3] http://rankings.ft.com/businessschoolrankings/global-mba-ranking-2015

[4] http://www.eduniversal-ranking.com/business-school-university-ranking-5palms.html

regard to the knowledge or skills required to run a business effectively, let alone commercialise an entirely new product or service. In my opinion, and I table this as nothing more than my personal viewpoint, several these qualifications equip would-be entrepreneurs with something that is quite harmful: Just enough knowledge and skill to believe that they are equipped for the task, but not enough to be successful. I also want to emphasise that I am not saying that one cannot be an entrepreneur without an MBA or a world-class MBA, I am merely using this as a proxy for the general state of our commercial qualifications. In other words, if many our MBAs are so poor by international standards, then what value do the rest of our business qualifications offer would-be entrepreneurs?

I noted earlier that education and experience are proxies for knowledge and skill and that they are not the same thing. Sadly, our qualifications are often poor or very poor proxies for knowledge and skill. Regretfully, these comments might come across as harsh, and I freely admit that, but I believe that it is a reality that we must face if we are serious about using entrepreneurship as a tool for driving economic growth and job creation. The quality of what we call entrepreneurship (and of course there are many exceptions – just not enough), is poor. Whether we like it or not, we are competing with the rest of the world both for capital and for market share, and if we do not up our game, we will lose. Trying to find quick and easy solutions so that we can avoid facing the real issues and harsh realities are only going to aggravate the problem. Unfortunately, the mediocre quality of our commercial qualifications probably reinforces the ridiculous notion that a would-be entrepreneur is more likely to be successful without a formal qualification simply because the marginal value of our formal qualifications is so low. The solution is not to throw out the baby with the bath water and abandon efforts to educate ourselves, but rather to fix the quality of these qualifications so that they add the requisite value.

I think we have established that we urgently need to address the skills shortage if we want to see a proliferation of entrepreneurs that are going to drive economic growth and before I get to the "how", I want to address a few fanciful myths about entrepreneurship. In doing so, the reader must allow me to move away from the objective and empirical for a moment. We will return to the objective shortly.

There is no magic involved in entrepreneurship. I obviously don't mean this in the literal sense, but because we haven't taken the time to understand entrepreneurship and its links to economic growth and job creation we have, metaphorically at least, created this mystical notion of something that is a silver bullet. Pouring large sums of money into something that we don't understand is not going to solve the problem and, as I have shown, is making the problem worse. Business owners themselves need to realise that being an entrepreneur is entering the harsh realities of business; of competing in a free market that judges the would-be entrepreneur only on the quality of their product or service. There is no magic, there is no single book that one can read that is suddenly going to transform the reader into Steve Jobs. To successfully run a business, one needs to understand how business works, the would-be entrepreneur needs to know how to manage their money, how to manage their people and how to be better than their competitors. This requires a very particular set of skills, and it is the responsibility of the would-be entrepreneurs to equip themselves accordingly. Would-be entrepreneurs love pointing out the fact that the likes of Steve Jobs and Richard Branson never went to university and they assume that entrepreneurs are superheroes that can be successful without an education. What they miss, is that you can easily count the number of entrepreneurs who were successful without a formal education, while it would take many books to list all the entrepreneurs who were successful because of their education. Secondly, the few individuals who were successful without any formal education were both exceptional and in many cases, very lucky. I recommend reading Malcolm Gladwell's *Outliers* on this subject. Unfortunately, popular culture has painted a very unrealistic picture of what we associate with the word entrepreneur. The entrepreneur is not a wheeler and dealer or some eccentric mad genius who conjures up wild schemes while making deals. Nor is the entrepreneur someone who runs around spewing out a bunch of poorly understood buzzwords to impress lesser mortals. The entrepreneur is a professional individual who understands business in all its complexity, can manage their staff well, consistently delivers superior value to their customers by efficiently combining factors of production, grows their business through constant innovation and in doing so earns a superior return that is greater than their cost of capital.

The hard truth is that by definition, most would-be entrepreneurs are not exceptional. Not only is this true by construction – by definition there can only be a very small number of exceptional people, but the evidence speaks for itself. How have many of these would-be entrepreneurs succeeded without the required knowledge and skills? We need to demystify entrepreneurship and turn down the volume on the hype. If we want to increase the number of successful entrepreneurs and if entrepreneurs want to increase their own success at an individual level, we need to equip ourselves with the right knowledge and skills to do so.

I will not test the readers' patience by straying from the objective any further, so let us return to how.

We need to promote what I call commercial skills and improve the quality of these commercial skills. The primary responsibility for this rests, I believe, not with the government, but with the would-be entrepreneur. No athlete is going to run the comrades or try out for the Olympics without training for it. No would-be entrepreneur should risk capital - theirs or an investor's - without making sure that they have the knowledge and skills to employ that capital productively. There are many ways to do this and going to business school is only one of them. I do not suggest that you cannot acquire the knowledge and skills without going to business school, but it is not going to happen automatically.

The above argument notwithstanding, we do live in a society that is horribly scarred by an atrocious past that we cannot ignore and that we cannot change. As a result of this past, there are an overwhelming number of individuals that neither have the commercial skills required to be successful, nor the means of acquiring them and if the market is not going to address that, then the government will have to. The solution is to address the root of the cause, not to make money available to those who are not equipped to employ it productively. This is like handing out free motorcars to everyone who cannot afford one and hoping that they'll learn to drive by trial and error – not a solution. First, teach them to drive and then help them to buy a car.

We need an intervention of quality, commercial skills.

In my opinion, there are two major ways to do this, and neither are perfect, but the first is better.

5.1.1   Market-led response: A less imperfect solution

The first is a market-led response and the second is a government-led response. The market-led response is better because it will be decentralised, will address specific local needs and will be more efficient.

Given the political tension at the moment I must pause for a moment to quantify my notion that the private sector is more efficient than the public sector. This comment is timeless and is not a comment about the current government. I am not writing this book from a political point of view. Across the world, including the so-called developed world, governments are less efficient than private enterprise. There are two major reasons for this. The first is that governments don't have a profit motive and their performance is generally measured by metrics that do not drive efficiency (if it is measured at all). The second is that governments that are democratic are not designed for speed, they are designed for collaboration towards reaching consensus. From an economic point of view, this tends to be inefficient.

The market-led response will require a social-entrepreneurship point of view, but there is no reason why it cannot be measured by a metric of value creation, in fact, it should be. This will require an entrepreneurial response to identify the specific local need and to develop an innovative response to commercialise the supply of that need.

It is as impossible to propose a solution to each situation as it is possible for one individual to develop a business plan for each type of business. What I table, therefore, is only an example of a possible response to demonstrate that a market-led response is both possible and feasible.

The notion of supplier development in our BBBEE codes is an example of where to begin. Again, I must quantify that I am supporting the notion of supplier development and not commenting on BBBEE. Supplier development is a "Lean" concept developed by Toyota, not a BBBEE concept.

A large organisation identifies a need within their supply chain that, if met, presents the organisation with an opportunity to be more profitable and create more value for their stakeholders. The fact that there is a demand in their supply chain might suggest (and for the purpose of this example we will assume that it does) that there is currently no entrepreneur meeting that demand. The organisation then identifies a would-be entrepreneur that is willing to try and meet this demand. The organisation understands that they cannot just give this potential supplier a chunk of capital and hope for the best. That would be an irresponsible use of the company's money. They rather develop a well-thought-out strategy to develop this entrepreneur. This could include assigning one of their managers to help the would-be entrepreneur set up the organisation and to coach him/her and the employees. They could employ the services of a business incubator to help with the development of the would-be entrepreneur and their team, and they could supply staged funding to finance the business or assist the start-up in securing funding. There are two key elements here, however. The first is not only active but proactive involvement in the development of the would-be entrepreneur and their staff. The second is that this must be handled as an investment that expects an economic return that is higher than the cost of the capital employed. I must emphasise that this is possible.

The reason for this, amongst others, is that the risk is closely managed and therefore the cost of capital is significantly lower than it would otherwise be.

This example is not novel, and I cannot claim credit for developing it. There are also many possible hybrids of this example, as well as many other possible examples.

5.1.2 The government-led response when the market fails

The government-led response is a more generic approach, and I'm pleased to say that it is being done. We need more colleges that teach entrepreneurship. I am hesitant to say teach entrepreneurship, because of the fuzzy concept that entrepreneurship has taken on in our use of the word. Entrepreneurship is not just teaching someone how to develop a business plan. It is teaching people how to plan a business, execute on that plan, run the business and constantly reiterate this. This also entails equipping the would-be entrepreneur with all the knowledge and skills to do this. This would include training in the disciplines that I suggested earlier when I introduced the concept of commercial skills. This is what I mean by teaching entrepreneurship. One of the critical elements of success in such training, I believe, is the completeness of the set of skills taught. We cannot just offer accounting courses (as an example) and say that we are training entrepreneurs. A successful entrepreneur is going to need the full set of skills.

The next issue is that of quality. Quality in education is a multidimensional concept, and in business education, I believe that it centres on the quality of the course material, the quality of the facilitator, the relevance of the course material, the degree to which the entire course is applied rather than purely theoretical and the opportunity to put the learning into practice. A key component of this is the nature and quality of the assignments given to the student/learner. A multiple-choice exam or the simple regurgitation of theoretical concepts is futile, and I believe that this approach is one of the major factors undermining the quality of much of the business education in the market. The quality of the facilitator goes hand in hand with this. The course will not have a relevant and practical component if the facilitator doesn't have the knowledge and skills acquired through both quality studies and practical experience. I emphasise this because the experience must be experience at doing the right thing and getting it right, not just many years of mediocre experience. It does not help to pass on knowledge and skills that are of inferior quality.

This last point brings us to the next challenge. Finding the appropriate human capital to train entrepreneurs. The solution is quite simple: Buy it and if necessary, import it, but before we do that, define exactly what we need. This will be one of the best investments in entrepreneurship that we can make.

The final ingredient for quality is time. I do not believe that one can effectively give a one-week course in entrepreneurship, nor can one give an effective one-month course in entrepreneurship. It is impossible to specify only one successful model for a course in entrepreneurship, but I believe that a very good model is a part-time one where the student/business owner has time to go back into their job/business and apply what they have learned. I don't think that anything less than a year will give sufficient time to cover what must be covered to give the would-be entrepreneur sufficient opportunity to apply this in their business. I offer this as an opinion and not as a rule.

5.2 A STRATEGY FOR IDENTIFYING AND DEVELOPING TECHNICAL SKILLS

The development of technical skills, as I defined them, would use similar approaches to developing them, but we have yet to return to which technical skills. As stated, I am not going to be presumptuous enough to list all the technical skills that we need to develop. I will rather discuss how we need to identify which technical skills need to be developed. I have mentioned that to do this, we must identify the potential competitive advantages we possess as a country. There are several concepts that we must understand to do this.

5.2.1 Theory of comparative advantage: How to identify a sector for technical skills development

While Prof Michael Porter of Harvard University is known for developing the model for determining National Competitive Advantage, it was economist David Ricardo who developed the theory of comparative advantage in the early 19th century. The essence of this theory is that nations should focus on producing what they are the most efficient at producing and trade with other nations to obtain goods that other nations can produce more efficiently. The best, simplified explanation can be found in Adam Smith's writings:

"If a foreign country can supply us with a commodity cheaper than we ourselves can make it, better buy it of them with some part of the produce of our own industry employed in a way in which we have some advantage. The general industry of the country, being always in proportion to the capital which employs it, will not thereby be diminished, but only left to find out the way in which it can be employed with the greatest advantage."

In essence, we want to do our best to employ our finite capital in the most productive way possible, and in doing so, we will enjoy the greatest return on that capital.

Ricardo's theory has a few problems with it, not the least of which he only considers trade between two countries. It is less simple to rank how productive we are compared to all our trade partners in each industry. One of the ways for doing this is to allow free trade without trade barriers or tariffs to allow the market to determine who supplies a product or service in the most efficient manner in much the same way as the domestic market is regulated by supply and demand.

The point is that we want to focus on allocating capital to the most productive sectors of the economy. The reader might already sense that I am inclined to suggest that capital will automatically find its way to the most productive sectors based on free market principles. This is correct, and I would be, but for the fact that our current policies are causing market distortions and that future effort might distort the markets even further. By this, I mean that if we start developing human capital in a sector of the market where we have less potential to be efficient, we will distort the market in that direction. More importantly, we don't want to be developing human capital in sector A when sector B holds more promise of a competitive advantage and capital is going to flow more freely to sector B, resulting in a huge pool of unemployed or underemployed human capital in sector A.

I do not suggest that we identify potentially competitive sectors so that we can artificially allocate capital to these sectors. If they are truly competitive, then the capital will flow there automatically. I suggest that we identify potentially competitive sectors that we can develop human capital in so that we can see capital flow there and benefit from increased entrepreneurship in these sectors.

5.2.2 Balancing the tension between creating economic growth and creating jobs

There is a second consideration, and that is the question of how much promise in terms of economic growth and job creation each sector offers since not all sectors are equal in this regard. The reader will remember that economists were divided on whether economic growth automatically led to job creation and that, earlier on, I stipulated that this link was not automatic. As we will see, some sectors are more labour intensive and thus hold more promise of job creation, while other sectors are more efficient and hold more promise of economic growth. There is often a trade-off between the two, and we need to be very sure that we understand this and the balance between what we can achieve and what we want to achieve. The reason that we need to make a trade-off is that we have several competitive advantages, more than we can develop at the same time. As with any good strategy, I would recommend that we pick the top two or three sectors and focus the bulk of our efforts in these. The sectors would be chosen for their competitive advantage, their promise of contributing to economic growth and their promise of job creation. Ideally, we would want a sector where we are the best in the world, the return on capital is 5% greater than the cost of capital, and the job creation coefficient is three to one, that is a 3% increase in the number of jobs for every 1% increase in GDP. Obviously, this is unrealistic.

To understand the balance between a sectors' potential contribution to economic growth and its contribution to job creation, we must understand the particular drivers of each.

We have seen that economic growth is a function of productivity. Productivity in its most simple form is the amount of output that we achieve for a given input and is thus given by the equation:

$$P = O/I$$

Where:

P = Productivity

O = Output

I = Input

Our return on capital is thus a good measure of productivity. If we take the total positive return on capital (after subtracting the cost of capital) and divide it by the capital employed we are left with not only our return on capital as a multiple but also our productivity with that capital:

$$Pc = ROC/TC$$

Where:

P_c = Productivity of Capital

ROC = Return on Capital

TC = Total Capital Employed

The productivity of an enterprise or industry will thus determine not only how attractive that enterprise or industry is for capital, but also the contribution to economic growth.

The relationship between productivity and job creation is a little more complicated. Since labour (as a factor of production) is employed by working capital, it is implied that the more productive labour is, the greater the absorption of labour. This is true when comparing organisations within a sector. The more productive an enterprise relative to its competitors or to the maximum level of productivity that an enterprise could achieve, the more likely it is to grow and create jobs.

When we compare different sectors and assume that each sector achieves its maximum level of productivity, we find that the less productive the sector is in terms of its labour, the higher the labour absorption of that sector will be. If we compare agriculture that is highly labour intensive and relatively unproductive with its labour when compared to the technology sector, we will find that the agricultural sector absorbs more labour. Thus, not only is productivity, in general, a key factor in determining the contribution to economic growth, but labour productivity is key in determining job creation. It is not, however, the only factor. Another critical factor is labour intensity. Labour intensity is sector-dependant when productivity is held constant. What this means is that if we assume labour productivity to be equal, then the overriding determining factor for labour absorption or potential job creation is the labour intensity of that industry.

The economy is typically divided into three sectors - primary, secondary and tertiary. These are roughly correlated with the factor-driven economy, the efficiency-driven economy and the innovation-driven economy. As noted, however, the definitions are different.

The primary sector of the economy is the sector that makes direct use of natural resources and includes mining, agriculture, forestry and fishing. The secondary sector produces manufactured goods, and the tertiary sector is the service sector.

Factor-driven economies use substantial amounts of unskilled labour, and natural resources and companies compete on prices since their products are typically non-beneficiated commodities. Efficiency-driven economies are driven by increases in productivity and product quality through superior techniques and processes. This sector makes less use of unskilled labour and more use of semi-skilled and skilled labour. The innovation-driven economies are those that are characterised by new products and services which are typically produced using the most sophisticated technology and processes. The innovation-driven economy uses substantial amounts of skilled labour and very little unskilled labour.

As a general rule, we can correlate these three continuums as follows:

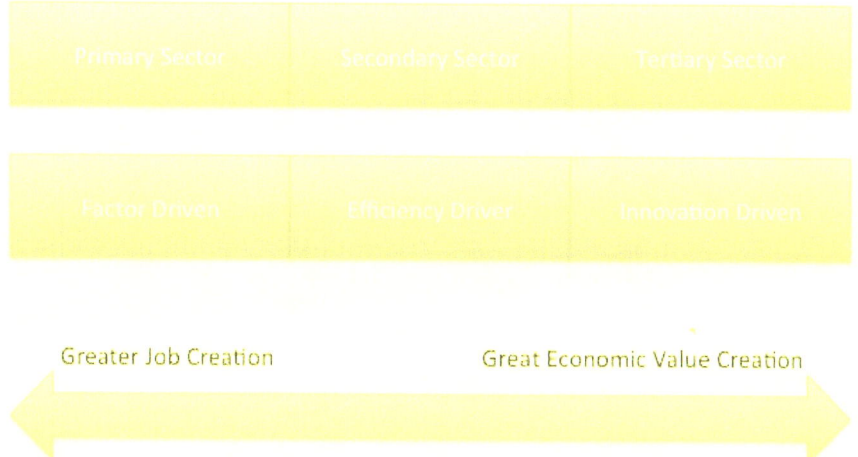

Figure 14: Correlation between various sectors and either contribution to economic growth or job creation

Once again, I emphasise the caveat that the correlations are not perfect. Tourism is a notable example of a blended sector that is primarily a service industry that can absorb substantial amounts of unskilled and semi-skilled labour. It is not particularly innovative and makes use of natural resources (scenery, game reserves, beaches) which are consumed by the tourist in the economic sense. What we do see is that there is often a trade-off between the contribution to economic growth and the contribution to job creation. To be sure, any enterprise that wants to create jobs must create economic value, but the amount of value created is often at odds with the number of jobs created. This is not because job creation detracts from economic growth. It is rather a function of the productivity of the jobs created: The less economically productive the labour, the smaller the contribution to economic growth.

We can represent this with a conceptual 2x2 as follows:

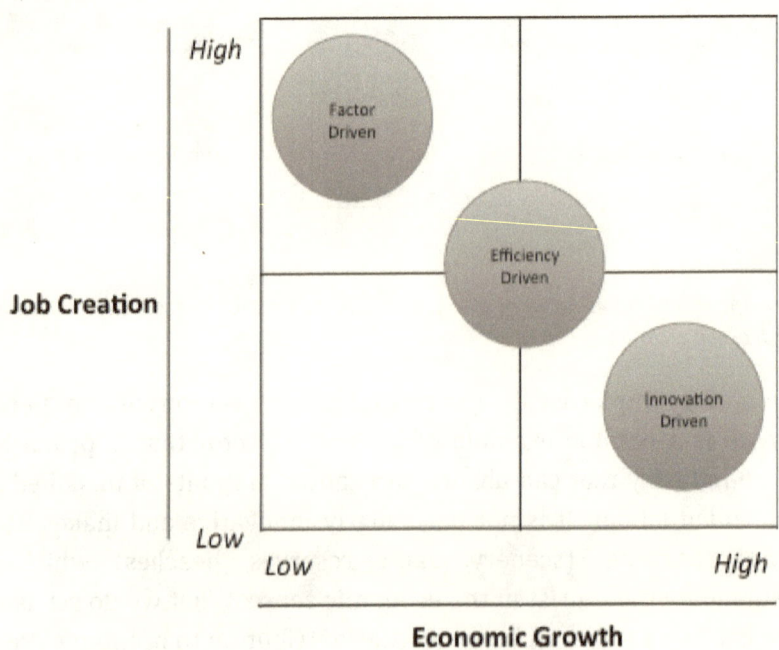

Figure 15: Balance between economic growth and job creation

This gives us a good framework for understanding how the development of technical skills will contribute to our efforts to promote economic growth and job creation. By increasing both the volume and quality of human capital in our economy, we will do two things. We will better equip entrepreneurs with the tools that they need to be successful, and we will provide them with a crucial type of capital that they can employ. The better the quality of this human capital, the more productive their businesses will be and the lower the risk. As a result, not only will we reduce the cost of financial capital (making it more accessible), but also the returns on that capital. The combination of reduced cost and increased returns will have a significant impact on the economic value created by these entrepreneurs and will also increase their demand for labour as their businesses grow. We understand that there is a potential trade-off between maximising the creation of economic value and maximising the creation of jobs, but we also understand that these goals are not mutually exclusive and that the promotion of successful entrepreneurship will achieve both, albeit to varying degrees.

5.3 Conclusion

We have seen that access to financial capital is critical to the success of any entrepreneur. We have also seen that many would be entrepreneurs struggle to access this financial capital for their businesses. More importantly, we have understood that a major reason for this is the lack of appropriate human capital for entrepreneurial success. We have understood that if we supply financial capital in the absence of the appropriate human capital needed to employ the financial capital productively, we will probably end up destroying economic value rather than creating it. In this case, even if jobs are created in the short-term, these will be short-lived, and in the long run, there will be a further increase in unemployment.

I suggest, therefore, that it is more prudent for us to focus on developing human capital that is appropriate for the areas in which we wish to achieve entrepreneurial success. This will be determined by understanding the areas where our economy can potentially enjoy a competitive advantage and by understanding how these areas will contribute to economic growth and job creation respectively. Over and above this, we need to significantly increase our investment in developing what I have termed commercial skills of an appropriate quality so that our would-be entrepreneurs are better equipped to employ the technical skills in an economically productive manner.

5.4 THE ELEPHANTS IN THE ROOM: UNPRODUCTIVE AND INFLEXIBLE LABOUR

This book would be incomplete without addressing two serious issues that pertain to our competitiveness as an economy and the ensuing impact that these have on our ability to create economic growth and create jobs. These are minimum wage and inflexible labour laws.

5.4.1 Minimum wage

One of the major potential competitive advantages that South Africa has is that it has an enormous supply of unskilled and semi-skilled labour that can not only be employed but easily up-skilled once in the workforce. I emphasise this last quantification, as it is critical. It is, unfortunately, beyond the scope of this book, so I will only touch briefly on it. Up-skilling labour is very critical in an emerging market as it allows us to continuously increase the productivity of our labour. This not only increases our economic growth but also makes way for new labour to enter the labour force as the employed labour becomes more productive and moves into more productive sectors of the economy. Up-skilling labour is not only easier and cheaper when labour is employed, but it happens automatically. This is because skills are acquired through experience. Thus, the exclusion of labour from the labour force not only decreases our economic growth but increases the cost of investing in human capital.

The problem is that unskilled labour is generally less productive than more skilled labour. It isn't unproductive, but less productive. This means that it generates a smaller return than more skilled labour. As a result of this, we can afford to allocate less working capital to unskilled labour. This results in lower wages. This economic reality is not only a festering wound in our collective psyche as a nation, but was the major point of contention for writers such as Karl Marx. Unfortunately, exploitation is a reality that we cannot simply ignore. The answer to exploitation has been a legislated minimum wage. I want to point out that such a concept is not opposed to free market principles. Adam Smith supported a similar concept regarding a ceiling on interest rates to prevent exploitation. Smith's writings also emphasised the need for the labour to earn sufficient to meet all his (or her) basic needs. Smith emphasised that such a restriction on the markets should be designed to prevent exploitation rather than to interfere with free markets. By definition, a free market wage would be a wage that an individual would freely choose to work for, rather than be forced to work for because of exploitation.

To be sure, minimum wages are necessary to prevent exploitation. Unfortunately, when minimum wages are set above the price level at which a free and fair market would clear, they automatically exclude people from the labour force, and they erode the competitive advantage of the economy. In economic terms, when the minimum wage is set above the value of the full return of labour then that labour will not be employed.

We have already seen that the exclusion from the labour force is pernicious, not only because it prevents people from being employed, but because it prevents them from gaining skills through experience that will enable them to be more productive and command higher wages in future. In addition to this, it seriously limits our competitive advantage as an economy. This is because we freely trade with other developing economies where wages are significantly lower than ours. Thus, not only do we indirectly endorse wages in other economies that are below our own minimum wage and what we would consider to be exploitive wages, but we do this at the cost of local jobs and local economic growth.

The moral dilemma aside, I am not proposing that we do away with minimum wages. What I am highlighting is that there is an enormous cost to our ability to grow the economy, up-skill our human capital, make the economy more productive and not only create more jobs but better-paying jobs. I highly recommend, *Why Africa is Poor* by economist Dr Greg Mills for further reading on this subject, which I can only highlight, but not address in detail.

5.4.2 Inflexible labour

The next issue is that of inflexible labour do due to inflexible labour legislation. I suspect that my response will be a surprise to most readers.

Inflexible labour is often cited as a major obstacle for entrepreneurs in South Africa. The problem that I have with these data is that all the research (that I have read) relies on survey-level data, which is opinion based. Is our labour really that inflexible? I do not believe that it is.

I have owned several companies in my life, and I have managed companies since I was in my late teens. Some of these have been start-ups (cash-strapped, resource-strapped and all the difficulties associated with a start-up) and some of them have been large. I also have a large network of colleagues and friends that include executive managers, entrepreneurs and small business owners. I have hired many people, and sadly, I have had to retrench and dismiss a few. I have never had a case go to the CCMA or Labour Court. I have managed my employees well – closely where necessary and, when performance has been sub-optimal, I have managed it accordingly. More often than not, I have not had to fire people because their performance has improved because of following the processes stipulated in our labour law. Where I have had to dismiss people, it has been at the end of a fair process that was genuinely designed to help them. The colleagues and friends of whom I speak all share similar experience. I do not doubt that our experience of the labour laws leads us to believe that they are inflexible, but I believe that this perception is based on the general inability of business owners and managers to manage their employees.

I believe that the following are contributing factors:

- The paucity of skill means that we struggle to find the right people for the job and end up hiring the wrong people.
- The paucity of skill means that even when we have hired the wrong person, finding someone to replace them is not easy.
- Large business owners and managers do not have the knowledge or experience to manage people correctly and as a result employees' performance is typically sub-optimal.
- When addressing deficient performance, business owners and managers don't have the knowledge or experience to rectify it.
- When the times comes to dismiss someone, there is a general ignorance regarding the process that must be followed, and this is compounded by a history of poor management that makes it difficult to put a fair case together.

My opinion therefore and I emphasise that it is my opinion, is that the perceived inflexibility of the labour law has its origins in poor management skills in general.

This does not mean that it isn't a problem. I believe that in general, the lack of strong management skills is a major barrier to successful entrepreneurship, but I believe that we have covered this extensively.

5.4.3 The inability of government to provide a business environment that is conducive to successful entrepreneurship

Hitherto I have emphasised the human capital aspect as a major problem with regards to successful entrepreneurship, and I hold to this. Notwithstanding, however, I would be remiss in not addressing the other major constraint of entrepreneurship: The failure of the government to provide an environment that is conducive to successful entrepreneurship. To be clear, this is dealt with in greater detail by other outstanding authors such as Dr Greg Mills, and I strongly recommend his latest work (co-authored with Jeffrey Herbst) "How South Africa Works and Must Do Better) to my readers. I address this glaring issue at a macro-level with broad brushstrokes, while Herbst & Mills address this in detail with outstanding case studies.

The current situation in South Africa presents nothing short of a crisis for entrepreneurship. Even the shortage of human capital, the challenges of minimum wage and issues with inflexible labour whether perceived or real are direct products of the lack of leadership in South Africa. Furthermore, the difficulties that are created by this lack of leadership exacerbate the problem of human capital. While there is undoubtedly a shortage, the challenges and obstacles put in the way of entrepreneurs and would-be entrepreneurs by the government mean that a higher level of human capital is needed to produce successful entrepreneurship than would otherwise be required. This means that several would-be-entrepreneurs would become successful entrepreneurs in a less challenging economic environment and many successful entrepreneurs would be significantly more successful if they did not face the challenges that they face.

It is ironic that government looks to "entrepreneurship" as a solution to the unemployment crisis and yet almost every action of government undermines the ability of would-be entrepreneurs and entrepreneurs to be successful. It is even more ironic that government is seeking to increase the supply of financial capital to the SMME sector to promote entrepreneurship while failing to recognise two crucial points. The first, we have seen, is that increasing the supply of financial capital to a sector that is unable to earn returns greater than the real cost of capital destroys economic value. The second is that one of the reasons that the cost of capital in South Africa is so high and that SMMEs and entrepreneurs struggle to access such capital is because of the extremely difficult business environment that has been created by governments' failure of leadership.

One might ask how this is the case. Quite simply, the myriad of difficulties that the private sector faces in doing business in South Africa reduce both the chances of success for the majority of businesses and the returns of the few that are successful. This increases the risk of doing business in South Africa, which in turn increases the cost of capital. This increase in the cost of capital reduces the total investment available in the economy and, in particular, to the most risk sub-sector of the private sector.

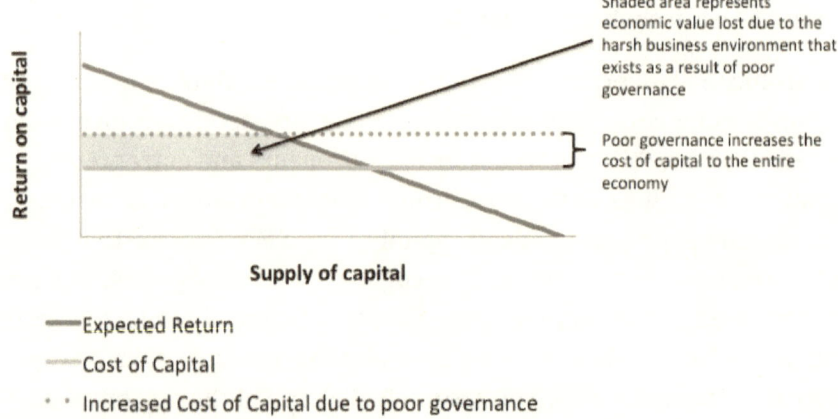

Figure 16: Government's contribution to destroying economic value

Artificially increasing the supply of capital available is the easy part and provides useful misdirection from the root cause of the problem. Unfortunately, as we have repeatedly seen, this approach is not only *not* a solution, but it destroys the value that we are trying to create. As we will see in more detail chapter seven, the most important thing that government can do to promote entrepreneurship is to govern well and focus on creating an environment that is conducive to successful entrepreneurship and one that is investor friendly. For as long as government fails to do this, we will continue to sub-optimal entrepreneurship at best.

6 Chapter Six: The rest of the story

Before we can develop a model for promoting entrepreneurship that will lead to economic growth and job creation, we need to understand that our situation is more complex than I have hitherto portrayed it. Unfortunately, the cost of capital is only part of the story. Regarding the cost of capital, we need to explore other costs of supplying capital including transactional costs and administrative costs. Regarding investment as part of our circular-flow model, we also need to explore exports and imports in more detail to understand their impact. Additionally, we need to understand a concept that has been discussed briefly, and that is the importance of value chains. Finally, we need to understand the cost of unemployment to society so that we can evaluate our cost of capital relative to this rather than absolutely. We cover these topics in this chapter.

6.2 COST OF CAPITAL, ONLY PART OF THE STORY

The supply of capital, whether through direct investment or loans is a business in its own right. As such, the cost of capital that arises from the risk is only part of the cost of running such a business. The most obvious other costs are the administrative expenses that are associated with supplying capital. These are essentially the running costs of running the business and include salaries, rent for premises and all the other costs associated with running a business. These costs are passed on to the users of capital through administration charges and interest. Most of these costs are fixed in nature (salaries, rent, etc.) and can, therefore, be diluted by administering large amounts of capital.

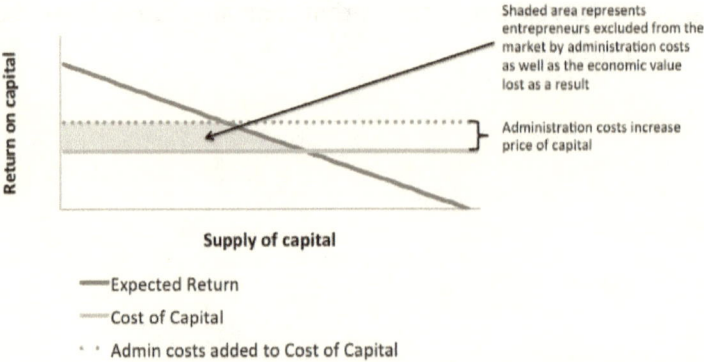

Figure 17: Entrepreneurs excluded from the economy due to administrative expenses

This makes the administration of smaller loans and investments significantly costlier. Typically, this makes finance more expensive for start-ups and small businesses than for larger existing businesses that typically use larger sums of capital – even if the cost of capital is held constant.

The next expense arises from what we call the asymmetry of information. This is slightly more complex because, while it is a separate concept, it drives both the administrative expenses and the cost of capital. For this reason, it is difficult to distinguish as a discrete expense. We will first understand what it is and then we will look at its effect on the other two expenses.

Asymmetry of information is a financial, economic term that describes the different levels of knowledge about a situation or firm between a supplier of capital and a consumer of capital. The concept can be traced back to Adam Smith's *Wealth of Nations* where he discusses how a large bank is less likely to know the creditworthiness of its borrowers than a smaller bank that has more personal contact (I'm paraphrasing). The more the supplier of capital knows about the consumer of capital the more they can manage their risk. Asymmetry of information drives up the administrative expenses in that resources are needed to gather information about a potential investment or borrower. This expense of information asymmetry is thus typically manifested in the administrative costs. Furthermore, the mere existence of information asymmetry increases the risk, which in turn drives the cost of capital.

The reader can personalise the situation by imagining a choice between buying shares in a new venture started by a well-known friend who is known to be a highly successful entrepreneur and who has just secured a highly lucrative contract and buying shares in the business of a stranger with no track record who has just secured the same contract. The second is clearly a higher risk than the first, and if we are going to buy shares at all, we are going to expect a bigger share in the company that we would of the friend who we trust.

In our context, the asymmetry of information is typically very high with start-ups and small businesses that do not have a strong credit record. Even if the owner has a strong personal credit record, this tells the would-be investor or lender very little of their ability to successfully run a business. This increases the effort required for a due-diligence process, driving the administrative expenses up, as well as the risk of such an investment or loan, driving the risk-related cost of capital up.

These costs can typically be very high – especially when diluted by small values. In *Capital in the 21st Century* Thomas Piketty shows that the returns on large investments are typically higher than on smaller investments. This is because of both of these factors:

Large investments typically have greater dilution effects of the due diligence, and administrative aspects and large portfolios can manage their risk better through diversification.

This increase in the total cost of capital over and above the risk-related cost of capital is a very real hurdle that would-be entrepreneurs face. This translates into a very strong counter argument to my suggestion that increased funding and subsidised funding can destroy economic value. It is not the only counterargument.

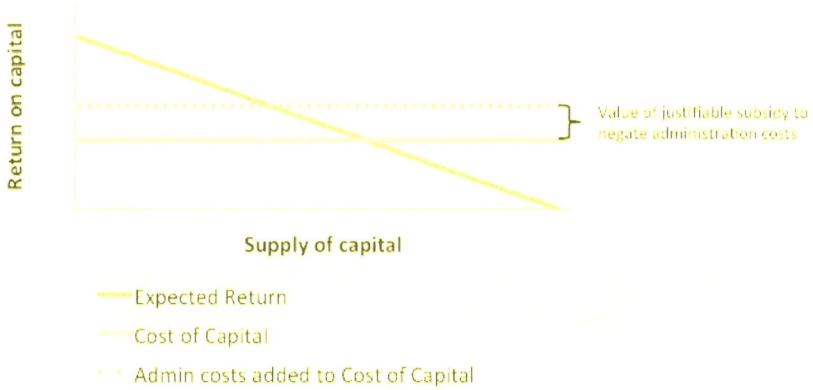

Figure 18: Justifiable subsidy based on administration costs

6.3 How long?

Another real-world challenge to the cost of capital argument is the timeframe in which we expect a return on our capital. Regardless of the departure point, it is completely unrealistic that any entrepreneurial venture, whether a new business, a new product or service, or an expanding business will earn its cost of capital from the beginning. This does not mean that it cannot earn its cost of capital over time.

Sasol would be an outstanding example of this. Sasol required massive investment. Not only this, but the risk involved was high. Sasol was the first company in the world to commercialise Coal to Liquid Fuel (CTF) technology, and the risks involved were enormous. As such, the cost of capital was extremely high. This, combined with the sheer volume of capital that was required made it an entrepreneurial non-sequitur in the conventional sense. It would have taken years for Sasol to earn its risk-related cost of capital and yet, there is no doubt today that Sasol has created significant economic value and several thousand jobs.

To be fair, there are not too many Sasol type examples, and typically investments of this scale do attract the right human capital and financial capital, but the example is still valid for smaller ventures.

Typically, the time frame in which it is expected that a loan will be repaid puts enormous cash-flow pressure on any entrepreneurial effort. While increasing the time frame for the repayment of a loan increases the risk, and therefore the cost of capital, increasing the time frame for repayment also eases the cash-flow pressures on the venture. In many cases, this increases the likelihood of success and both long-term value creation and sustainable job creation.

It is important to understand that by increasing the timeframe in which the investor or lender expects their capital and its returns to be paid can help to solve the administration costs and information asymmetry costs as well. These costs will still be borne by the consumer of capital, but over a time frame that is feasible in terms of cash-flow.

6.4 AN IMPERFECT SOLUTION

The first and correct response to both challenges should be a market response. On the assumption that there is a large number of potential entrepreneurs who could be successful if they were only given longer-term access to financial capital, then there must be a sufficiently profitable market for such funding. Clearly, I would not be writing this if such a market existed. The obvious question is, why?

The obvious answer is that the assumption is flawed and that there are insufficient would-be entrepreneurs who have the appropriate human capital to be successful in the market for longer-term capital.

The reader might have guessed that I support this view – at least in part. I would not go so far as to say that there are none, but I do believe that there are insufficient to create a wholesale market for longer-term entrepreneurial credit. I do believe that there are sufficient potential entrepreneurs for a niche market and I believe that there is scope for the development of new financial products to serve these potential entrepreneurs. Unfortunately, one of the major barriers to this innovation is subsidised capital.

Subsidised capital presents a barrier to financial innovation in the following ways:

6.4.1 Competing with private enterprises in the provision of capital

We have already covered this, and I won't rehash the points that we have covered. It is important to understand that a provider of longer-term entrepreneurial capital would need to balance their financial portfolio with less risky shorter-term funding. We have already seen that subsidised capital is reducing the private sectors' market share in this area and thus driving out investors.

6.4.2 Too many moths around the flame

By making financing easier to come by, more seekers of capital are encouraged to enter the market. Ostensibly this is precisely the goal. Unfortunately, however, most of the entrepreneurs that would have been successful would have already accessed free market funding. What is left over are the would-be entrepreneurs who, with their current paucity of human capital, are most likely will-never-be entrepreneurs that are not going to contribute to economic growth and sustainable job creation. By increasing the number of capital seekers in the market, we make the search for successful entrepreneurs that much more difficult and increase the chances of financing an unsuccessful venture. This, in turn, increases the aggregate risk, increases the cost of capital and discourages market-led innovation.

I would recommend that subsidies and grant funds rather be allocated to existing financial institutions which will manage the funds for profit but under the mandate of allocating these to entrepreneurial ventures as longer-term funding. In my opinion, this would need to be coupled with the withdrawal of subsidised funding and a concerted effort to develop potential entrepreneurs through programmes that not only develop skills but quality skills that are appropriate to the entrepreneurial opportunities. These "appropriate skills" would include both commercial skills and the relevant technical skills.

It is beyond the scope of this book, but I believe that the very best way of doing this would be partnerships between financial institutions, larger corporates seeking to develop their supply chains and the relevant providers of training. The financial institutions would use the funding supplied to them as discussed above, to provide finance to would-be entrepreneurs selected to an identified need in a supply chain of a larger corporate. The larger corporate would reduce the risk of the investment by providing both a contract and added support through coaching and mentoring. The external service providers could provide formalised training with appropriate courses. The funding for the training could be financed through a number of ways. One of them could be as part of the overall funding for the venture, the other could come out of the CSI budget of the corporate or it could be subsidised in the short-term. Whatever the funding model for the human capital development aspect, it must be accounted for the entire cost of the investment and offset against the returns on the investment. The payback period could be longer than conventional investments, but should not exceed a reasonable time frame. Ultimately, the long-term returns should exceed the total cost of capital.

I must emphasise two important caveats with the above example: Firstly, it is extremely rudimentary and generic. It is neither novel nor groundbreaking, but rather a simple conceptual example to demonstrate the possibility of developing market-led solutions to our current dilemma. Secondly, it is only one example. I do not even begin to suggest that there are no other, more innovative and productive ways to solve this problem – and I would encourage academics, policy-makers and practitioners to take up the challenge of developing models that can address the needs of all stakeholders – including the providers of capital. In addition to the above caveats, I must stress that supply chains are not the only areas that offer a realistic opportunity for developing entrepreneurs.

6.5 Other important considerations from our circular-flow model

Returning to our circular model

$$GDP = C + I + G + (X - M)$$

We have dealt extensively with Investments (I), but have not dealt with Government Spending (G), Exports (X) and Imports (M) in the same detail.

We will deal with exports and imports first and return to government spending later.

6.5.1 Exports and imports

Exports and imports are, from an economic point of view, the same thing on opposite sides of the equation, one is positive, and the other is negative. This is why we add the net of exports and imports to our circular-flow equation. When talking about exports and imports, we are in fact talking about the revenue from exports and the expenditure on imports. When viewed in this way, exports are an inflow of money for the economy and imports are an outflow from the economy. In this simplistic sense, we want to export more than we import. I must emphasise that this is a massive over-simplification and it is primarily based on the assumption that foreign trade (exports and imports) is a result of free market trade. What this means is that because of supply and demand forces, we will export only products and services that offer more value to the end-user (in a foreign country) than they can get from anywhere else in the world. As with standard market principles, this would mean that we can either supply superior quality products or services or that we could supply product and services of comparable quality at a lower price. Similarly, we would import products and services that are cheaper to import than to make locally. We would import them from a country that could offer the best value.

With the free market assumptions holding true, it means that we would want to export more than we import as this would mean that we are more productive. We have seen that it is productivity that leads to economic growth. As soon as the free market principles are interfered with through trade barriers, tariffs or subsidies, the assumption fails to be true and exports are not necessarily better than imports. Protectionism through subsidies, tariffs and trade barriers has been a topic of debate among policy makers and economists for decades. I will summarise by saying that as with the dilemma that we found with creative destruction, where jobs are created at the expense of others, the issue of globalisation offers similar challenges. To be sure, international free trade leads to economic growth, but often at the expense of certain jobs within an economy. This is one of the reasons that minimum wage not only impedes economic growth but also destroys jobs. Due to globalisation, we are competing against countries like China and India that have an almost unlimited supply of cheap labour. Protectionism is often used to protect local jobs, and these intentions are not only noble but also not unique to Africa. The United States (to mention only one developed world country) has often resorted to protectionist policies. Unfortunately, however, the short-term benefits of protectionism always come at the expense of economic growth and long-term sustainable job creation. As with the process of creative destruction, entrepreneurship is not only a crucial as an enabler of economic growth and job creation but also a critical catalyst in helping an economy adjust to changes in the labour market due to innovation and globalisation.

Returning to exports and imports that assume that for the most part, free market principles hold. It should be clear that exports are more desirous than imports. It is important to understand that exports are a result of greater productivity and in this sense, our focus remains on increasing productivity. We must be careful to not make exports a goal for the sake of exports in much the same way as we must guard against pursuing a proliferation of SMMEs for the sake of it. Exports should be a natural result of increased productivity. Notwithstanding, however, if we are going to identify investment opportunities with respect to developing human capital and promoting entrepreneurship, then by doing so in a sector or industry where we can competitively either export or substitute imports (which has the same effect), then we have the added benefit of earning foreign revenue (or decreases foreign expenditure) which will contribute to economic growth.

All of this is, of course, elementary, I mention it, however, because there is a critical role for government to play here that does not include subsidies. We return briefly to the assumption about free market exports, namely that we can supply superior value to the end-user in a foreign country (through superior quality at a competitive price). This is where the government has a role to play. Many of the inefficiencies that add unnecessary cost to both our exports and domestic product (resulting in imports of goods and services that are cheaper than they can be produced locally) and prevent entrepreneurs from being competitive globally are factors entirely beyond the control of the entrepreneur. These include the inefficient infrastructure such as the bottlenecked ports and clearing houses, the high manufacturing costs due to the unreliable power supply, etc. All of these erode the competitiveness of entrepreneurs and potential entrepreneurs to the point where they are unable to compete globally.

The government would do far better in promoting entrepreneurship, economic growth and job creation by focusing on governing well and efficiently than they could ever do through providing subsidies to SMMEs that will probably only add to the inefficiency of the economy.

I would go so far as stating that if the government wants to promote entrepreneurship, then the only thing that they need to focus on is governing well. This would include:

- Improving the reach and quality of our education system.
- Reducing crime[5].
- Maintaining existing infrastructure such as the railways and our energy utility[6].
- Eliminating corruption[7].

---

[5] A broad range of research has shown that crime increases the cost of doing business and deters investment.

[6] No comment is needed on our energy crisis, but it should be highlighted that the need to transport goods via road because of the inferior quality of our railway system is a major detractor from the competitiveness of the entire economy by driving up the cost of everything either directly or indirectly. This reduces our purchasing power and destroys economic value. When considering entrepreneurs and would-be entrepreneurs, this added expense just decreases the potential competitiveness of any business and further destroys value.

[7] Corruption not only deters investment, but has a major effect of destroying entrepreneurship.

I do not want to labour these points, but I would be remiss in not pointing out that this is where the government should focus its efforts. Allocating funds from subsidising human-capital-starved-SMMEs doomed to operate in an inefficient business environment hallmarked by crime and corruption is a shortcut to destroying economic growth and jobs. Reallocating these funds to address fundamental issues of good governance (even if only the four issues that I have outlined) will do more to promote entrepreneurship than the current subsidies could achieve. It will also increase our ability to export and reduce our need for imports.

Returning specifically to exports and imports, it is important to understand that increased productivity will automatically result in increased exports and decreased imports, over and above increased investment. We know that all three of these will lead to economic growth.

6.5.2 Government spending

In Keynesian economics, government spending is one form of kick-starting an economy that is in a downturn. In this sense, government spending has the same effect as increased investment in an economy and leads to economic growth. In our local context, government spending has been targeted at SMMEs and in particular, at those with appropriate BBBEE ratings. There are many problems with this approach, and the first should be clear to the reader by now. The government spending is not targeted at entrepreneurship, it is targeted at SMMEs with strong BBBEE credentials. I have mentioned earlier that I am not going to debate the merits and demerits of BBBEE since the focus of this book is on entrepreneurship. Unfortunately, the approach of selecting SMMEs on any criteria other than those for entrepreneurial success as we have defined it are not only not going to promote entrepreneurship that leads to economic growth and job creation but runs the risk of promoting SMMEs that destroy economic growth and jobs in the long run. This is a function of what we have already understood and is not directly linked to BBBEE *per se*.

The other problem with the current focus of government spending on SMMEs is that it has neglected the original goals of both economic growth and job creation and has assumed, incorrectly, that the goal is the proliferation of SMMEs. We understand that this assumes that a proliferation of SMMEs leads to economic growth, but we have also seen that this assumption is wrong. Even if this assumption were correct, it is unnecessary. From our circular-flow model, we see that government spending is directly linked to economic growth due to the multiplier effect. There is, therefore, no need to try to promote economic growth indirectly by targeting SMMEs when government spending is directly linked to economic growth. The problem arises with the fact that the assumption is flawed and that government funds are being spent on SMMEs that destroy economic growth. As we have seen, this has the effect of cancelling out the benefits that we would have enjoyed. To achieve economic growth, government spending should be targeted at projects that deliver a positive economic return. This will give us not only the benefit of the multiplier effect but also the benefit of the positive return on capital.

The next important aspect when considering government spending is the question of what it is spent on. This is not the same as which business it is used to employ (discussed above), but rather the actual service or product that it is used to purchase. We have seen that one critical role that the government needs to play in promoting entrepreneurship is to make the economy, as a whole, a more efficient environment for entrepreneurs to operate in. If for example, we can reduce our transport costs by putting more goods on rail and reducing idle time in our ports, we will lower the overall cost of delivering a product to the global market. Another example would be the ability to achieve a cost-effective and reliable supply of electricity. This would lower the costs of doing business in our economy, would make entrepreneurs more productive and would dramatically increase both economic growth and job creation beyond the actual spend itself. Thus, we can see that government spending can go beyond both its direct effect on economic growth through the multiplier effect and contribute to GDP by being spent on entrepreneurs who generate positive economic value by employing the capital productively. Government spending can increase overall economic productivity and thus, contribute further to long-term economic growth. We will classify this as productive spending. If we have productive spending, then it follows that there must be unproductive spending. My example for this wins no points for originality but is one that all readers will understand well: Nkandla. Given the examples of the railways, ports and electricity, it should be easy to understand that government spending on projects such as Nkandla do nothing to make the economy more efficient for entrepreneurs to operate in. If we leave the scandalous controversy aside for a moment and treat Nkandla as nothing more than a presidential homestead, then we see that it does nothing to make the economy a more efficient place for entrepreneurs to operate. It is an unproductive asset and therefore classified as unproductive spending. Unfortunately, this example does nothing for investor confidence and by discouraging investors from investing in what is perceived to be a corrupt economy, destroys entrepreneurship and in turn, economic growth and job creation. It is important for the reader to understand that it is impossible for a government to have no unproductive spending. To be sure, security upgrades are necessary for a presidential residence, as are government buildings and other such unproductive assets. It is extremely important, however, to recognise that unproductive spending should be limited as far as possible and that the focus of government spending should be on productive assets.

6.5.3   Government grants

Thus, far I have argued that any entrepreneurial venture needs to earn a positive return on its capital after accounting for the cost of capital. We have seen that this is an unreasonable expectation in the short-term for any start-up and that the current investment horizons are often too short and that it is worthwhile extending these to allow start-ups a better chance of earning their cost of capital in the long run. We have also seen that there is an argument for subsidies that can ameliorate the administration costs for smaller investments, but only to the point where the return that an enterprise is paying to the supplier of capital equals or nearly equals its cost of capital.

What we have not yet considered is the economic cost of social grants because of unemployment. There is no economic return for a social grant provided to an unemployed person – the capital is not productively employed and thus no direct benefit is purchased. This is then, another form of unproductive government spending. Again, it is sadly necessary, but we need to understand how it is economically and socially viable to limit it. Any increase in productivity achieved on capital spent on government grants would be more economically beneficial than the current situation.

Again, I am not suggesting that we cancel social grants and divert these funds to investing in entrepreneurs. What I am suggesting is that every job that is created that employs an individual who is currently receiving a social grant in such a way that they are no longer in need of the grant adds the full benefit to the economy of the saved grant. This is a very important when considering the overall cost of capital to the economy. It is also very easy to calculate the direct benefit to the economy, as is it equal to the value of the grant that is no longer paid. On this basis, we can justify a subsidy of capital to the entrepreneur that is equal to the value of social grants that will be saved by their venture.

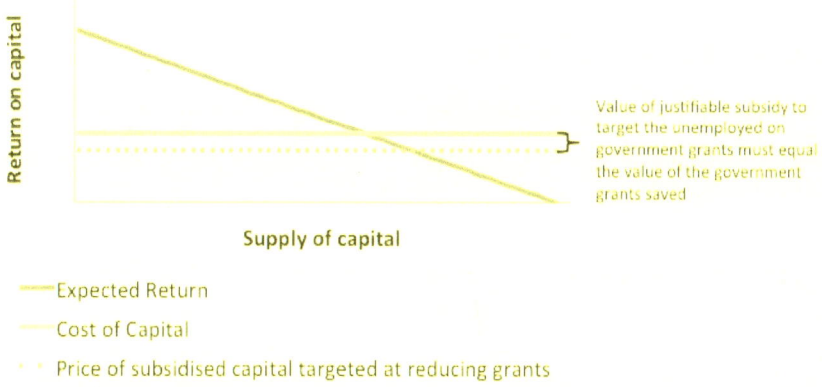

Figure 19: Justifiable subsidy should equal the value of government grants saved

It is also important to remember that inclusion in the labour force increases the human capital of the employed through experience. For this reason, this situation is preferable as it increases the total human capital of the economy, which can be employed more productively at a later stage. Hope is also placed on the possibility that such subsidised ventures will earn more than their cost of capital in the long run and thus, the net result will be economic growth.

6.5.4   Explaining the importance of developing value chains

I have referred to the development of value chains several times, but have hitherto not explained the importance thereof. Value chains are important because of both the multiplier effect and the synergies that they can offer when focusing on economic development.

The multiplier effect is important because the same money that is spent at the end of a value chain will find its way through the entire chain to the beginning. Thus, these value chains provide us with an opportunity for multiple opportunities to create economic value and to create jobs with the same investment. The other important aspect of value chains is that synergies exist between suppliers and their customers who are lower down in the chain. These synergies, if exploited, have the potential to increase the productivity across the entire value chain and contribute further to economic growth. Unfortunately, many of the potential synergies in existing value chains are not currently being exploited, this, however, does not nullify the argument for synergies within the supply chain. What it does do is emphasise the need for human capital that can help us exploit these.

We have already seen that the potential for creating entire value chains in our economy is an important consideration when focusing our efforts on developing appropriate human capital.

7 Chapter Seven: Conclusion and Recommendations

We have understood so far that our goal is to reduce unemployment and that economic growth is a necessary enabler of this, but that job creation is not an economic consequence of economic growth. We know now that as important as economic growth is, it is not enough to only achieve economic growth, but that job creation needs to keep pace with the economic growth to ensure that wealth of the economy is better distributed.

Economic growth in terms of an increase in GDP per capita is a function of productivity and that if we want to achieve economic growth, we need to become more productive. Gains in productivity are achieved through various kinds of innovation which we have defined as the successful commercialisation of a new product, service, idea or business model. These innovations are brought about by entrepreneurs who employ factors of production in the pursuit of profit. The entrepreneur needs a specific type of human capital namely commercial skills (sometimes called entrepreneurial capital) to combine the other factors of production successfully. These factors of production include *inter alia* financial capital and labour. When employing financial capital, the entrepreneur incurs risk, which in turn affects the cost of the financial capital employed. The labour employed by the entrepreneur includes the concept of human capital that we have understood (albeit imperfectly) as technical skills. We have seen that if the quality of the human capital offered by labour is more productive, the more productive the enterprise can be, the lower the risk and the greater the returns. Similarly, the better the quality of the commercial human capital or entrepreneurial capital, the more productive the enterprise, the lower the risk and the greater the returns. The difference between the returns on capital and the cost of capital determine the contribution (when positive) or detraction (when negative) from economic growth. When positive, these returns are called Economic Value Added or EVA®. EVA® is, therefore, a measure of how productively the total capital (financial and human) of the enterprise is employed by the entrepreneur.

For this reason, we do not want to invest in businesses that do not generate a return greater than their cost of capital. This has led us to understand the difference between SMMEs, entrepreneurs and the understanding that we want to increase the supply of entrepreneurs demanding capital, rather than the supply of capital to SMMEs. To achieve this, we should be focusing on improving the supply of both the human capital needed to successfully combine factors of production and the human capital that can be employed as productive labour. In developing this human capital, we have seen that the development of commercial human capital required to combine the other factors of production is generic and agnostic of industry, but that in developing what we defined as technical human capital, we need to be strategic and focus on those sectors that offer us the best competitive advantage, whilst balancing the results between economic growth and job creation. This can be done by diversifying our efforts between the innovation-driven economy and the efficiency and factor-driven economies which are more labour intensive. Furthermore, we need to focus on building value chains within these sectors so that we can leverage the synergies and the multiplier effect for added economic benefit.

With regards to subsidised financing; while it is clear that no effort should be made to subsidise the risk-related cost of capital, there is scope for a subsidy to remove the administrative costs of smaller investments. Notwithstanding, it is my recommendation that these funds be administered through the private sector by means of public/private partnerships.

With regards to government spending we have seen that, as with increasing the supply side of funding available to SMMEs, our current focus of government spending on SMMEs rather than on entrepreneurs that can create economic value is destroying value rather than creating it. Furthermore, we have seen that government spending should, as far as possible, be focused not only on entrepreneurs but on projects that will make the economy as a whole, a more productive environment for entrepreneurs to operate in. This would include minimising unproductive spends, such as unproductive projects and social grants. This redirection of government spending should not undermine the social justice provided by government grants, but should rather focus on job creation opportunities that mollify the need for the grants. This reduction in unproductive government spending would justify the subsidisation of initiatives that focus on creating employment amongst consumers of government grants, to the value of the government grants that would be saved.

Overall there is a desperate need to increase the number of entrepreneurs who can create economic growth and contribute to job creation. While there is a need to address the transactional costs associated with financing smaller entrepreneurs and start-ups, the main problem is the shortage of these entrepreneurs. The overarching solution, I believe, is to increase the quality of human capital in our economy as we have discussed. Not only is increasing funding to SMMEs that do not possess this human capital, not a solution, but it is also completely counterproductive. Furthermore, our current business environment is one that is extremely unproductive and possess several challenges for even the best entrepreneurs.

The solution as I see it is for the government to refocus its efforts away from wantonly providing funding and contracts to SMMEs and to focus on developing quality human capital in a targeted manner, governing well and spending responsibly on projects that will have a productive benefit to the economy at large.

If we want to address unemployment, then productive entrepreneurship can be a tool to achieve this. I believe that the following seven-point model will assist us in developing a more effective strategy:

7.1 ADOPT A GREATER FREE MARKET APPROACH REGARDING FUNDING

Ultimately, capital needs to be employed by those who can employ it in the most productive manner. This is how we are going to maximise both economic growth and job creation. The government should redirect its funding away from financing SMMEs to other areas that can contribute more to entrepreneurship.

Furthermore, the government should focus on policy that attracts entrepreneurs and investors to the economy and strengthens the current investment environment within the economy.

7.2 FOCUS ON DEVELOPING QUALITY COMMERCIAL SKILLS WITHIN OUR ECONOMY

We need to increase the number of service providers that are providing quality entrepreneurial training within our economy and drastically increase the quality of commercial education provided by current suppliers. This will involve *inter alia:*

7.2.1 Improving the quality of primary and secondary schooling

We cannot shy away from the fact that there are serious problems with our primary and secondary schooling. While the increase in the matric pass rate has been applauded in some circles, the matric results neglect to highlight the fact that students are taking easier subjects and that this is making it easier to pass. They also neglect the fact that the mark needed to pass matric is substantially lower than international standards. Finally, the pass rate completely ignores the fact that more than 50% of secondary school learners drop out before reaching matric. There is little hope of equipping would-be entrepreneurs with the correct knowledge and skills if half of our secondary school learners do not even get to matric and only 70% of those who do pass a matric that is not worth the paper it is written on.

7.2.2 Raising the standard for accreditation of commercial/entrepreneurial courses

The Council for Higher Education is responsible for the accreditation of qualifications within the South African economy. The accreditation standards should be revised to be brought in line with international standards and, as far as commercial/entrepreneurial programs go, these should include:

- The quality of faculty delivering the courses including not only their academic qualifications but also their level of successful practical experience.
- The quality of the course material and assignments.
- The practical application of the course including, but not limited to the assignments.
- The entrance criteria for applicants (as appropriate to the course). A key factor in this will be the overall improvement in primary and secondary schooling.

7.2.3 Public/Private Partnerships

For the first time, I will guard against simply stating that the private sector will supply better education than the public sector can simply because the evidence will refute such a statement. Our strongest universities are all government institutions, and I cannot think of one completely private tertiary institution that offers a commercial qualification anywhere near on par with our top government universities. Notwithstanding, I believe that our private primary and secondary schools tell exactly the opposite story. Furthermore, there are many government universities that provide sub-standard qualifications. I believe that there is an enormous market for innovative models that will provide high-quality entrepreneurial education to the market. I believe that there is huge scope for public/private partnerships in this market since starting up such institutions is very costly and providing purely private education to those who most need it, is, for the most part, unaffordable.

7.2.4 Improving the quality of government institutions that provide commercial/entrepreneurial education

I have already applauded the fact that there are a handful of government institutions that provide better than world-class commercial education. Unfortunately, there are not enough. Many have fallen from delivering outstanding qualifications to delivering mediocre qualifications at best. There is a serious need to address the quality of commercial education in our universities. This will be achieved by:

- Improving accreditation standards (as discussed).
- Making faculty and management appointments on merit.
- Increasing salaries of faculty and management to attract the best talent.
- Importing the very best talent that we can afford where necessary.

7.2.5 Exploit opportunities for entrepreneurial development within value chains

I have already covered an example of this in Chapter Five, and I have emphasised that it is only one example. What I want to emphasise is that this is a major area where the private sector has a responsibility to promote entrepreneurship. This is not to say that the private sector is not shouldering this responsibility, but I do believe that there are a lot more opportunities that can be exploited. The private sector must accept that it is in their own interests to promote economic growth and job creation within our economy. In accepting this responsibility, they should do everything they can to identify opportunities for developing entrepreneurs within their area of influence. These areas might possibly be outside of their own value chains, but I believe that the greatest number of opportunities will lie within their value chains. By focusing on new and existing developing entrepreneurs within their value chains, the private sector can create shared value that will not only benefit the entrepreneurs but also their shareholders.

In line with the above proposition, I believe that there is an enormous demand for providers of high-quality business development services and business incubators to partner with organisations that are looking at developing entrepreneurs and providing the coaching and training required. While this is currently being done – mostly in the pursuit of BBBEE points - I believe that the private sector needs to move beyond simply pursuing scorecard points and start actively pursuing innovative ways to create shared value.

What I must emphasise again, is that in all of these opportunities need to create value. I am not suggesting subsidising projects that do not deliver economic value. What I am suggesting is that there should be far more opportunities to create value while developing new and existing entrepreneurs than we are currently doing.

7.3 FOCUS ON DEVELOPING QUALITY TECHNICAL SKILLS IN SECTORS THAT HOLD POTENTIAL FOR ACHIEVING OUR GOALS

As far as the quality of technical skills goes, everything that I have said previously about commercial skills is also applicable to technical skills. One added emphasis, however, is the critical need for an improvement in Math and Science amongst matriculates.

I believe that there is in fact, little to be said for identifying the areas where we have a competitive advantage as an economy. I think that a huge amount of good work has been done. What we need to focus on is rapidly developing quality skills in these areas and specifically improving the quality of the skills development projects that we have.

One of these sectors is the industrial sector, and for this sector, we need to drastically increase the number of engineers and artisans within our economy.

Another sector in which we need to rapidly develop human capital is the agricultural sector. Our infamous neighbour is the world-leading example in how to destroy an agricultural sector by allocating agricultural capital to individuals who have not been equipped with the skills to make that capital productive.

Finally, and I believe one of the most important for our economy, is an investment in hospitality skills and skills needed for the tourism industry which I will discuss as a separate point.

7.4 FOCUS ON DEVELOPING THE TOURISM INDUSTRY

The tourism sector in Africa is one that makes use of one of the factors of production that we have not really spent much time discussing. That factor is natural resources. Unlike mining and agriculture, these resources are consumed in a way that they are not exhausted. That might sound confusing, but in economic terms consumed does not literally mean that they are consumed. It means that the consumer uses them. Natural resources such as our wildlife, beaches and Table Mountain can, therefore, be consumed (in the economic sense) by tourists without being depleted. This could be referred to as natural capital. What this means is that we can use these factors of production in the same way that we would use normal capital without investing as much financial capital. This means that the return on capital (or economic value added) of this sector is potentially higher. Furthermore, the human capital requirements in the tourism industry are typically less specialised and less costly. Another advantage of this sector is that it has long value chains. If one thinks of an inbound tourist, they will typically fly in. Not only are they (hopefully) making use of our local airlines, but they are also using our airports where they will pay passenger taxes, eat at a restaurant, and possibly use a taxi or shuttle service. They will almost certainly utilise accommodation that they pay for whether it is a hotel, guesthouse, or game farm. During their stay, they will make use of many services that could include taxis, tour guides, suppliers of recreational activities, restaurants, etc. Each of these suppliers, in turn, has a value chain that enjoys the revenue earned from the tourist. The added benefit is that much of this revenue is foreign. Thus we are increasing our exports at the same time.

In terms of developing the tourism industry, I am not suggesting that we provide subsidised capital. There is a huge amount that the government can do to promote this sector. This includes not only the development of relatively cost effective human capital previously discussed, but also governing well and increasing productive government spending on infrastructure related to tourism. These are discussed below.

7.5 Focus on Governing Well

One of the most important, yet neglected roles of government in promoting entrepreneurship is the need for government to govern well. In addition to the education system, which we have already discussed, the critical elements that need attention are:

7.5.1 Corruption

Corruption kills entrepreneurship in many ways:

- It scares off investment, both foreign and domestic.
- It allocates resources unjustly and typically away from entrepreneurs who would earn the greatest return on capital. The need to secure contracts by means of corruption suggests that the contract would not be secured on merit in the first place.
- It decreases the productive spend of government.

7.5.2 Crime

Crime not only scares off investors but also increases the cost of doing business in an economy. It also deters tourism, which as we have seen is currently one of our most important industries.

7.5.3 General efficiency

I have already stated that governments are typically inefficient. This does not mean that governments can be as inefficient as they like. I believe that the general inefficiency of our government is much worse that it either could or should be. It is beyond the scope of this book to detail how the government could be more efficient, but I will emphasise that the inefficiency of government in their role adds to the inefficiency of the economy which decreases the economic value added of all entrepreneurs. It also increases the value destruction of businesses that are not able to create value. An example of where we have done well does exist - The South African Revenue Services. They ensured that South-Africans become tax compliant and their process was relatively efficient. We need more examples of such efficiency in government.

7.5.4 Service delivery

Service delivery is a critical part of making the business environment optimal for entrepreneurs. This includes everything from keeping the country clean to keeping the lights on. Poor service delivery has a direct cost on the economy, it erodes the productivity of entrepreneurs and businesses alike, and finally, the major unrest that is resulting from poor service delivery is driving away investment and detracting from the productivity of the economy.

7.5.5 Legislative frameworks

One of the key functions of government is to enforce legislation, which means is to increase the cohesiveness and productiveness of society. Unfortunately, much of our legislation does little to increase the cohesiveness of our society but does a lot to harm its efficiency. This includes everything from making it difficult to import the critical human capital that we need, to making it extremely difficult for tourists to visit our country. All of this has a major impact on entrepreneurs' ability to create economic value and participate in sustainable job creation.

7.6 INCREASED PRODUCTIVE GOVERNMENT SPENDING

We have covered sufficient examples to understand why this is important. The reader also does not need to be reminded of the critical need for better productive spending on infrastructure such as reliable power utilities, railways, ports, and decent roads.

What must be emphasised is that productive spending is not only investment in productive infrastructure, but also responsible spending when doing so. Quite simply, the money needs to be spent without waste. This means that we need competent individuals managing this spend and the projects on which these funds are spent. This not only means that the service providers should be efficient to create economic value, but that the public servants who are managing these investments must be competent and responsible in the use and maintenance of these assets.

Once we are sure that we can spend responsibility we will do well to reallocate money that was earmarked to fund SMMEs and spend it responsibly on entrepreneurs who are able to provide productive infrastructure and assets.

The other critical way to increase the productive government spending is to reduce unproductive government spending. This not only means minimising spend on unproductive efforts, but it specifically means reducing wasteful government spending due to incompetence and corruption (which often go hand in hand).

7.7 FOCUS ON SUBSIDISED INITIATIVES THAT WILL GET THE UNEMPLOYED INTO THE JOB MARKET

We have seen that another way of reducing unproductive government spending is to reduce the spending on social grants. I have emphasised that this needs to be done without undermining the social justice provided by such grants. One way of doing this is to increase employment among those individuals that would typically receive a social grant. I have also shown that there is justification for subsidising such efforts to the value of the social grants saved. While in the short run, this nets out to the same value of the grant spending, it is marginally more productive. In the long run, the subsidy will have been saved, and the economy will benefit from the value add from the additional labour.

One of the tools that offer some promise in this regard is the informal sector. This is a sector that requires low levels of capital investment, in terms of both financial capital and human capital. Unfortunately, after much research on the matter, I have concluded that this sector has several drawbacks. Firstly, it is very difficult for those in the informal sector to break out of the sector into the formal labour sector. Secondly, the returns in the informal sector are very low, seldom providing an income that is above the breadline. For these reasons, the informal sector often reinforces the poverty trap.

I believe that a better response would be a range of apprenticeship programmes particularly targeted at unskilled unemployed. These apprenticeships need not only be artisanal in nature but could also include administrative work and opportunities in the agricultural sector. These would primarily be investments in human capital, rather than directly in entrepreneurship. I believe that the best and most efficient way would be to create tax incentives, like the youth wage subsidy for businesses that create these apprentice programmes. This would, like the youth wage subsidy, have the benefit of creating jobs, while supplying businesses with subsidised labour. The major challenge to this would be the issue of the minimum wage since the government grant (ironically) falls below the minimum wage. I do not doubt that with a small compromise on the minimum wage, we would find that the private sector will be willing to contribute wages over and above the subsidy for these positions. I must emphasise that I am tabling this as an example of a solution and not stating it as the primary solution.

7.8 Conclusion

It is beyond doubt that entrepreneurship as we have explored it is a promising tool for both economic growth and sustainable job creation. It is important for us to understand that it is only a means to an end (albeit a critical one), rather than an end in itself. Given our stated goal of addressing unemployment, it is necessary for us to accept the economic realities around how entrepreneurship can be part of the solution and to tailor our efforts according to these realities. If we do this, I believe that we can reverse the current damage that is being done and see a more prosperous and egalitarian society than we have ever known.

8 BIBLIOGRAPHY

ANC. (1955). The Freedom Charter. Retrieved from http://www.anc.org.za/show.php?id=72

ANC. (1994). Reconstruction and Development Programme (RDP, Base Document). Johannesburg, RSA: Umyanyano Publications.

Arko-achemfuor, A. (2012). Financing Small, Medium and Micro-Enterprises (SMMEs) in Rural South Africa: An exploratory study of stokvels in the Nailed Local Municipality, North West Province. *Journal of Social Anthropology*, *3*(2), 127–133.

Ashton, D. N. (2005). High skills: The concept and its application to South Africa. *Journal of Education and Work*, *18*(1), 19–32. doi:10.1080/1363908052000332294

Badroodien, A. (2005). Enterprise training in post-apartheid South Africa. *Journal of Education and Work*, *18*(1), 85–110. doi:10.1080/1363908052000332320

Baumol, W. J., Litan, R. E., Schramm, C. J., & Strom, R. J. (2011). Innovative entrepreneurship and policy: Toward initiation and preservation of growth. *The Economics of Small Businesses*, 3–23. doi:10.1007/978-3-7908-2623-4

Beck, T., & Demirguc-Kunt, A. (2006). Small and medium-size enterprises: Access to finance as a growth constraint. *Journal of Banking & Finance, 30*(11), 2931–2943. doi:10.1016/j.jbankfin.2006.05.009

Beck, T., Demirguc-Kunt, A., Laeven, L., & Levine, R. (2008). Finance, Firm Size, and Growth. *Journal of Money, Credit and Banking, 40*(7), 1379–1405. doi:10.1111/j.1538-4616.2008.00164.x

Beck, T., Demirgüç-Kunt, A., Laeven, L., & Levine, R. (2004). *Finance, firm size and growth* (No. 10983). Cambridge, MA.

Beck, T., Demirgüç-Kunt, A., Laeven, L., & Maksimovic, V. (2006). The determinants of financing obstacles. *Journal of International Money and Finance, 25*(6), 932–952. doi:10.1016/j.jimonfin.2006.07.005

Beck, T., Demirguc-Kunt, A., & Levine, R. (2005). SMEs, Growth, and Poverty: Cross-Country Evidence. *Journal of Economic Growth, 10*(3), 199–229. doi:10.1007/s10887-005-3533-5

Beck, T., Demirgüç-Kunt, A., & Levine, R. (2005). SMEs, growth and poverty: Cross-country evidence. *Journal of Economic Growth, 10*(3), 199–229.

Beck, T., Demirgüç-Kunt, A., & Maksimovic, V. (2005). Financial and legal constraints to growth: Does firm size matter? *The Journal of Finance, 60*(1), 137–177.

Becker, G. (1962). Investment in human capital: A theoretical analysis. *Journal of Political Economy, 70*(5), 9–49.

Berger, A. N., & Udell, G. F. (1998). The economics of small business finance: The roles of private equity and debt markets in the financial growth cycle. *Journal of Banking & Finance, 22,* 613 – 673.

Bhorat, H., Hirsch, A., Kanbur, R., & Ncube, M. (2013). Economic policy in South Africa: Past, present and future, 1–27.

Bloch, G. (2011). A Weak Foundation for Children.

Boeke, J. (1953). Economics and Economic Policy of Dual Societies. New York, NY: Institute of Pacific Relations.

Boone, A., & van Witteloostuijn, A. (1996). Industry competition and firm human capital. *Small Business Economics*, *8*(5), 347–364.

Bowen, D., & Hisrich, R. (1986). The female entrepreneur: A career development perspective. *Academy of Management Review*, *1*(1), 393 – 407.

Brockhaus, R. (1982). The psychology of the entrepreneur. In A. C. Kent, D. L. Sexton, & K. H. Vesper (Eds.), *Encyclopaedia of entrepreneurship*. Englewood Cliffs, N.J.

Bruhn, M., Karlan, D., & Schoar, A. (2010). What capital is missing in developing countries? *American Economic Review*, *May*, 629 – 633.

Bucci, A. (2005). *Human Capital, Product Market Power and Economic Growth*.

Buera, F. J. (2009). A dynamic model of entrepreneurship with borrowing constraints: theory and evidence. *Annals of Finance, 5*(3-4), 443–464. doi:10.1007/s10436-009-0121-2

Butler, D. (2006). *Enterprise planning and development – small business start-up and growth.* London, UK: Elsevier Butterworth and Heinemann.

Callaghan, C. W. (2012). The effect of financial capital on inner-city street trading. *Journal of Economic and Financial Sciences/ JEF/ April, 5*(1), 83–102.

Cantillon, R. (1755). *Essai sur la nature du commerce en général.* Retrieved from http://www.jstor.org/stable/3497121?origin=crossref

Carland, J. W., Hoy, F., Boulton, W. R., & Carland, J. A. C. (1984). Differentiating Entrepreneurs from Small Business Owners: A conceptualization. *Academy of Management Review, 9*(2), 354–359.

Cetorelli, N., & Strahan, P. E. (2013). Finance as a Barrier to entry: Bank competition and industry structure in local U.S. Markets. *The Journal of Finance, 61*(1), 437–461.

Chandler, G., & Hanks, S. (1994). Founder competence, the environment, and venture performance. *Entrepreneurship Theory and Practice, Spring*, 77 – 89.

Chandler, G., & Hanks, S. (1998). An examination of the substitutability of founders human and financial capital in emerging business ventures. *Journal of Business Venturing, 13*(5), 353 – 369.

Chandler, G., & Jansen, E. (1992). The founder's self-assessed competence and venture performance. *Journal of Business Venturing, 7*(3), 223 – 236.

Cooper, A., Gimeno-Gascon, F., & Woo, C. (1994). Initial human and financial capital as predictors of new venture performance. *Journal of Business Venturing, 9*(5), 371–395.

Craig, B. R., Jackson III, W. E., & Thomson, J. B. (2007). *Does government intervention in the small-firm credit market help economic performance?* Cleveland, OH.

Cressy, R. (1996). Are business start-ups debt-rationed? *The Economic Journal, 106*(438), 1253–1270.

Davidsson, P., & Honig, B. (2003). The role of social and human capital among nascent entrepreneurs. *Journal of Business Venturing, 18*, 301 – 331.

Demirgüç-Kunt, A., & Maksimovic, V. (1998). Law, Finance, and Firm Growth. *The Journal of Finance, 53*(6), 2107–2137.

Dess, G. G., & Robison, R. B. (1984). Measuring organisational performance in the absence of objective measures: The case of the privately- held firm and conglomerate business units. *Strategic Management Journal, 5*(3), 265 – 273.

Devereux, M., & Schiantarelli, F. (1990). Investment, financial factors, and cash flow: Evidence from U.K. panel data. In R. G. Hubbard (Ed.), *Asymmetric Information, Corporate Finance and Investment* (pp. 279–306). Chicago, IL: University of Chicago Press. Retrieved from http://www.nber.org/chapters/c11476

Dias, R., & Posel, D. (2007). *Unemployment, education and skills constraints in Post-Apartheid South Africa* (No. 07/120).

Dictionary O. E. (2006). *Oxford English Dictionary*. Oxford University Press.

Dollinger, M. J. (2008). *Entrepreneurship: Strategies and Resources*. (L. Rubenstein, Ed.) (4th ed.). Lombard, Illinois: Marsh Publications.

Drucker, P. (1985). *Innovation and entrepreneurship: practice and principles*. New York, NY: Harper & Row.

DTI. (2005). Integrated strategy on the promotion of entrepreneurship and small enterprises. Pretoria, RSA: Department of Trade and Industry South Africa.

DTI. (2013). Industrial Policy Action Plan. Pretoria, RSA: Department of Trade and Industry South Africa.

Duchesneau, D., & Gartner, W. (1990). A profile of new venture success and failure in an emerging industry. *Journal of Business Venturing*, 5(5), 297–312.

Emerson, J. (2000). *The nature of returns: A social capital markets inquiry into elements of investment and the blended value proposition*.

Erikson, T. (2002). Entrepreneurial capital: the emerging venture's most important asset and competitive advantage. *Journal of Business Venturing, 17,* 275 – 290.

Esther, N., & Mazwai, T. (2012). *Working Papers from the Third International Conference: Growing industries in townships and under-developed neighbourhoods.* Johannesburg, RSA: The Centre for Small Business Development of the University of Johannesburg, Soweto Campus.

Evans, D. S., & Jovanovic, B. (1989). An estimated model of entrepreneurial choice under liquidity constraints. *Journal of Political Economy, 97*(4), 808–827.

Fatoki, O. (2012). The impact of entrepreneurial orientation on access to debt finance and performance of small and medium enterprises in South Africa. *Journal of Social Science, 32*(2), 121–131.

Fine, D., van Wamelen, A., Lund, S., Cabral, A., Taoufiki, M., Dörr, N., ... Cook, P. (2012). *Africa at work: Job creation and inclusive growth.*

Fisher, I. (1930). *The theory of interest.*

Fisman, R., & Love, I. (2007). Financial dependence and growth revisited. *Journal of European Economic Association2*, *5*(2), 470 – 479.

Galindo, A. J., & Schiantarelli, F. (2003). *Credit Constraints and Investment in Latin American*. IDB.

Guiso, L., Sapienza, P., & Zingales, L. (2004). Does local financial development matter? *The Quarterly Journal of Economics*, (August), 929 – 969.

Harper, M., & Tanburn, J. (2005). Mapping the Shift in Business Development Services – Making markets work for the poor. Warwickshire: ITDG Publishing.

Hashi, I., & Krasniqi, B. a. (2011). Entrepreneurship and SME growth: evidence from advanced and laggard transition economies. *International Journal of Entrepreneurial Behaviour & Research*, *17*(5), 456–487. doi:10.1108/13552551111158817

Heilbrunn, S., Rozenes, S., & Vitner, G. (2011). A "DEA" based taxonomy to map successful SMEs. *International Journal of Business and Social Science*, *2*(2), 232–241.

Herrington, M., Kew, J., Simrie, M., & Turton, N. (2011). *Global Entrepreneurship Monitor 2011 Report: South Africa.*

Herrington, M., & Maas, G. (2006). *Global Entrepreneurship Monitor South African Report.* Cape Town, RSA.

Hodge, D. (2009). Growth, employment and unemployment in South Africa growth. *South African Journal of Economics, 77,* 488–504.

Imbs, J. (2013). The Premature De-Industrialization of South Africa.". *The Industrial Policy Revolution II: Africa in the 21st Century,* 529–540.

Jensen, M. C., & Meckling, W. H. (1976). Theory of the Firm : Managerial Behavior, Agency Costs and Ownership Structure. *Journal of Financial Economics, 3*(4), 305 – 360.

Kesper, A. (2001). *Failing or not aiming to grow? Manufacturing SMMEs and their contribution to employment growth in South Africa. Urban Forum* (Vol. 12). Johannesburg, RSA. doi:10.1007/s12132-001-0015-5

Keynes, J. M. (1932). Economic possibilities for our grandchildren. New York, NY: Harcourt Brace.

Keynes, J. M. (1936). *The general theory of employment, interest and money.*

Kim, W. C., & Mauborgne, R. (2005). *Blue Ocean Strategy: How to create uncontested market space and make competition irrelevant.* Boston, MS: Harvard Business School Press.

Kirsten, M. A. (2011a). Improving the well-being of the poor through microfinance : Evidence from the Small Enterprise Foundation in South Africa, (December).

Kirsten, M. A. (2011b). *Improving the well-being of the poor through microfinance: Evidence from the Small Enterprise Foundation in South Africa.* University of Stellenbosch.

Kraak, A. (2005). Human resources development and the skills crisis in South Africa: the need for a multi-pronged strategy. *Journal of Education and Work, 18*(1), 57–83. doi:10.1080/1363908052000332311

Kropp, F., Lindsay, N. J., & Shoham, A. (2008). Entrepreneurial orientation and international entrepreneurial business venture startup. *International Journal of Entrepreneurial Behaviour & Research, 14*(2), 102–117. doi:10.1108/13552550810863080

Kumar, K. B., Rajan, R. G., & Zingales, L. (1999). *What determines firm size?* (No. 7208). Cambridge, MA.

Leitner, K., & Güldenberg, S. (2010). Generic strategies and firm performance in SMEs: a longitudinal study of Austrian SMEs. *Small Business Economics, 35*(2), 169–189.

Lewis, W. (1954). Economic development with unlimited supply of labour. The Manchester School.

Li, Y.-H., Huang, J.-W., & Tsai, M.-T. (2009). Entrepreneurial orientation and firm performance: The role of knowledge creation process. *Industrial Marketing Management, 38*(4), 440–449. doi:10.1016/j.indmarman.2008.02.004

Ligthelm, A. (2006). An evaluation of the role and potential of the informal economy for employment creation in South Africa. *South African Journal of Labour Relations, 30*(1), 30–50.

Ligthelm, A. (2010). Entrepreneurship and small business sustainability. *Southern African Business Review*, *14*(3), 131-153.

Little, I. M. D., Mazumdar, D., & Page, J. M. (1987). Small manufacturing enterprises: A comparative analysis of India and other economies. Oxford: Oxford University Press.

Low, M. B., & Macmillan, I. C. (1988). Entrepreneurship: Past research and future challenges. *Journal of Management*, *14*(2).

Macpherson, A., & Holt, R. (2007). Knowledge, learning and small firm growth: A systematic review of the evidence. *Research Policy*, *36*(2), 172–192. doi:10.1016/j.respol.2006.10.001

Magretta, J. (2003). *What management is*. London, UK: Profile Books.

Marx, K. (1894). *Das Kapital, Kritik der politischen Ökonomie*. Verlag von Otto Meisner.

Mashigo, P. (2009). Transforming the South African credit market through group lending mechanisms. *Journal of Case Research in Business and Economics, 2*, 1–16.

Mayer, M. J., & Altman, M. (2005). South Africa' s economic development trajectory: implications for skills development. *Journal of Education and Work, 18*(1), 33–56. doi:10.1080/1363908052000332302

Mazanai, M., & Fatoki, O. (2011). The effectiveness of Business Development Services Providers (BDS) in improving access to debt finance by start-up SMEs in South Africa. *International Journal of Economics and Finance, 3*(4), 208–216. doi:10.5539/ijef.v3n4p208

Mazaqi, E. T. (2009). *The effectiveness of local business service centres in small business development: A study in Gauteng Province, South Africa*. University of Pretoria.

Mbonyane, B. L. (2006). *An exploration of factors that lead to failure of small businesses in the Kagiso Township*. University of South Africa, RSA.

Mbonyane, B. L., & Ladzani, W. (2011). Factors that hinder the growth of small businesses in South African townships. *European Business Review*, *23*(6), 550–560. doi:10.1108/09555341111175390

McGrath, S. (2005). "Skills for productive citizenship for all": The place of skills development for micro and small enterprises in South Africa. *Journal of Education and Work*, *18*(1), 111–125. doi:10.1080/1363908052000332339

MGI. (2010). *Lions on the move: The progress and potential of African economies*. Chicago, IL.

Mills, G. (2012). *Why Africa is Poor* (2nd ed.). London, UK: Penguin Books.

Mintzberg, H. (1987). Crafting strategy. *Harvard Business Review*, 66 – 75.

Morduch, J. (1998). Poverty, economic growth, and average exit time. *Economic Letters*, *59*(January), 385–390.

Mthente Research and Consulting Services (Pty) Ltd. (2012). *Analysis of the Needs, State and Performance of Small and*

Medium Businesses in the Agriculture, Manufacturing, ICT and Tourism Sectors in South Africa.

National Planning Commission. (2011). *National Planning Commission: Diagnostic Overview.*

National Planning Commission. (2013a). National Development Plan: Vision for 2030. *Pretoria, RSA: National Planning Commission.*

National Planning Commission. (2013b). New Development Plan Vision 2030.

Nattrass, N. (2011). The new growth path: Game changing vision or cop-out? *South African Journal of Science, 107*(3/4), 1–8. doi:10.4102/sajs.v107i3/4.638

Ndala, V. S. (2012). *Primary Contextual Factors: Vital Determinants for Sustainable Township Businesses and Industrial Development in South Africa.* (N. Esther & T. Mazwai, Eds.). Johannesburg, RSA: Working Papers from the Third International Conference: Growing industries in townships and under-developed neighbourhoods at the

Centre for Small Business Development of the University of Johannesburg, Soweto Campus.

Nkosi, E., & Bounds, M. (2012). *Skills required for the management of small enterprises in the retail sector in Soweto*. (N. Esther & T. Mazwai, Eds.). Johannesburg, RSA: Working Papers from the Third International Conference: Growing industries in townships and under-developed neighbourhoods at the Centre for Small Business Development of the University of Johannesburg, Soweto Campus.

O'Sullivan, S. (2003). *Economics Principles in Action (California Edition)*. Prentice Hall.

Oliner, S. D., & Rudebusch, G. D. (1992). Sources of the financing hierarchy for business investment. *The Review of Economics and Statistics*, 74(4), 643–654.

Orford, J., Herrington, M., & Wood, E. (2004). *GEM: South African Report*.

Pack, H., & Westphal, L. E. (1986). Industrial strategy and technological change: Theory versus reality. *Journal of Development Economics*, 22, 87–128.

Pagano, P., & Schivardi, F. (2001). *Firm Size Distribution and Growth,"* (No. 394).

Parsons, R. (2013). *Zumanomics revisited:* Johannesburg, RSA: Jacana Media.

Pauw, K., Oosthuizen, M., & Westhuizen, C. Van Der. (2006). Graduate Unemployment in the Face of Skills Shortages : A Labour Market Paradox. In *Accelerated and Shared Growth in South Africa: Determinants, Constraints and Opportunities*. Johannesburg, RSA: Development Policy Research Unit.

Pennings, J. M. (1998). Human capital, social capital, and firm dissolution. *The Academy of Management Journal*, *41*(4), 425–440.

Piketty, T. (2014). *Capital in the 21st Century*. (A. Goldhammer, Ed.). Cambridge, MA: Harvard University Press.

Pissarides, F. (1999a). Is lack of funds the main obstacle to growth? EBRD's experience with small- and medium-sized businesses in Central and Eastern Europe. *Journal of Business Venturing*, *14*(5-6), 519–539. doi:10.1016/S0883-9026(98)00027-5

Pissarides, F. (1999b). Is lack of funds the main obstacle to growth? EBRD's experience with small- and medium-sized businesses in Central and Eastern Europe. *Journal of Business Venturing*, *14*(5-6), 519–539. doi:10.1016/S0883-9026(98)00027-5

Porter, M. (1998). *The Competitive Advantage of Nations*. New York, NY: Free Press.

Republic of South Africa. Constitution of the Republic of South Africa, Act 108 of 1996 (1996). Government Gazette. Retrieved from http://www.gov.za/documents/constitution/1996/a108-96.pdf

Republic of South Africa. (1996b). *Growth Employment and Redistribution, A macroeconomic strategy*. Pretoria, RSA: Government Printer.

Republic of South Africa. Amendment of section 1 of Act 102 of 1996, as amended by section 1 of Act 26 of 2003 (2003). Republic of South Africa.

Republic of South Africa. (2010). The New Growth Path. Retrieved May 21, 2014, from http://www.gov.za/aboutgovt/programmes/new-growth-path/index.html

Ricardo, D. (1821). *On the principles of political economy and taxation* (3rd ed.). UK: John Murray.

Rittel, H. W. J., & Webber, M. M. (1973). Dilemmas in a general theory of planning. *Policy Sciences, 4*(2), 155–169.

Rodrik, D. (2014). An African growth miracle? Princeton, NJ: Princeton University.

Roemer, M., & Gugerty, M. K. (1997). *Does economic growth reduce poverty?*

Rogerson, C. M. (2004a). *Local Economic Development and post-apartheid reconstruction in South Africa* (Vol. 18). Johannesburg, RSA: Department of Geography & Environmental Studies, University of the Witwatersrand, Johannesburg, South Africa.

Rogerson, C. M. (2004b). The impact of the South African government's SMME programmes: A ten-year review (1994-2003). *Development Southern Africa, 21*(5), 765–784. doi:10.1080/0376835042000325697

Rogerson, C. M. (2008). *Tracking SMME development in South Africa: Issues of finance, training and the regulatory environment.* Johannesburg, RSA: Department of Geography & Environmental Studies, University of the Witwatersrand, Johannesburg, South Africa.

Rolfe, R., Woodward, D., Ligthelm, A., & Guimarães, P. (2010). *The viability of informal micro-enterprise in South Africa.* New York, NY: Presented at the Conference on ―Entrepreneurship in Africa,‖ Whitman School of Management, Syracuse University, Syracuse, New York, April 1-3, 2010.

Rumelt, R. P. (2011). *Good Strategy Bad Strategy: The Difference and Why It Matters.* New York, NY: Crown Business.

Schiffer, M., & Weder, B. (2001). *Firm size and the business environment: worldwide survey results.*

Schoombee, A. (1999a). Linkage Banking for micro-enterprises in South Africa. *South African Journal of Economics, 67*(3), 419 – 455.

Schoombee, A. (1999b). Linkage Banking for micro-enterprises in South Africa. *South African Journal of Economics, 67*(3), 419–455.

Schoombee, A. (2000a). *Banking for the Poor: The success and failures of South African banks.* Wellington, New Zealand: Paper read at the DEVNET conference on "Poverty, Prosperity and Progress" Victoria University of Wellington.

Schoombee, A. (2000b). Getting South African banks to serve micro-entrepreneurs: An analysis of policy options. *Development Southern Africa, 17*(5), 751 – 767. doi:10.1080/0376835002001360

Schoombee, A. (2000c). Getting South African banks to serve micro-entrepreneurs: An analysis of policy options. *Development Southern Africa, 17*(5), 751–767. doi:10.1080/0376835002001360

Schultz, T. (1961). Investment in human capital. *The American Economic Review, 51*(1), 1 – 17. doi:10.1126/science.151.3712.867-a

Schumpeter, J. (1942). *Capitalism, Socialism, and Democracy*. New York, NY: Harper & Bros.

Schwarze, C. (2008). Involving the accounting profession in the development of financial management skills of micro-enterprise owners in South Africa. *Meditari Accountancy Research, 16*(2), 139–151.

Sharpe, W. (1964). Capital asset prices: A theory of market equilibrium under conditions of risk. *Journal of Finance, 19*(3), 425–442.

Smith, A. (1789). *An inquiry into the nature and causes of the wealth of nations* (5th ed.). London, UK: W. Strahan and T. Cadell.

Stander, C. (2011). *Exploring women entrepreneurship in selected areas in South Africa*. North-West University.

Stern, J., Stewart, B., & Chew, D. (1995). The EVA financial management system. *Journal of Applied Corporate Finance, 8*(2), 32 – 46.

Stevenson, L., & Lundström, A. (2002). Beyond the rhetoric: Defining entrepreneurship policy and its best practice components. Swedish Foundation for Small Business Research [Forum för småföretagsforskning].

Strydom, J., & Tustin, D. (2004). Business skills of small businesses in the peri-urban areas of Northern Tshwane. In *Proceedings of the 49th International Council for Small Business (ICSB) World Conference – 20 to 23 June 2004.* Johannesburg, RSA.

Thurik, R., & Wennekers, S. (2004). Entrepreneurship, small business and economic growth. *Journal of Small Business and Enterprise Development, 11*(1), 140 – 149.

umJwali. (2012). *Research on the performance of the manufacturing sector.*

University of Chicago GSB. (1998). The origins of EVA. Retrieved from http://www.chicagobooth.edu/magazine/summer98/Stern.html

Venter, R., Urban, B., & Rwigema, H. (2008). Entrepreneurship: Theory in practice.

Visagie, J. C. (1997). SMMEs' challenges in reconstructing South Africa. *Management Decision*, *35*(9), 660–667. doi:10.1108/00251749710186496

White, S. (2004). Business Development Services policies, institutional frameworks and service delivery models: International good practice and lessons for South Africa. Johannesburg, RSA: Johannesburg: Southern African IDEAS (Initiatives for the Development of Enterprising Actions and Strategies.

Wickham, P. a. (2006). Overconfidence in new start-up success probability judgement. *International Journal of Entrepreneurial Behaviour & Research*, *12*(4), 210–227. doi:10.1108/13552550610679168

Xu, B. (1998). *A reestimation of the Evans-Jovanovic entrepreneurial choice model*. Gainesville, FL.

Zingales, L., Fama, G., Klenow, P., & Rodriguez-clare, A. (1996). *Financial dependence and growth* (No. 5758). Cambridge, MA.

www.ingramcontent.com/pod-product-compliance
Lightning Source LLC
Chambersburg PA
CBHW020905180526
45163CB00007B/2628